Insights on the Business Climate in Kazakhstan

OECD
BETTER POLICIES FOR BETTER LIVES

Please cite this publication as:
OECD (2023), *Insights on the Business Climate in Kazakhstan*, OECD Publishing, Paris, https://doi.org/10.1787/bd780306-en.

ISBN 978-92-64-95252-2 (print)
ISBN 978-92-64-95046-7 (pdf)
ISBN 978-92-64-59622-1 (HTML)
ISBN 978-92-64-81827-9 (epub)

Photo credits: Cover © Hairem/Shutterstock.com.

Corrigenda to OECD publications may be found on line at: www.oecd.org/about/publishing/corrigenda.htm.

Foreword

Kazakhstan is the largest economy in Central Asia, with growth primarily driven by the extraction and export of a narrow range of commodities that the country has in abundance. While the country's extractive sectors will continue to be important for the economy, the government has a long-standing commitment to economic diversification, with a mature, wide-ranging set of policies in place to achieve this. The commitment to diversification reflects the awareness that extractives-driven growth has created resilience challenges in the short-term due to the immediate impact of external demand shocks on domestic output, and that in a context of the net-zero transition, it cannot provide inclusive, sustainable growth in the long-term.

The country has emerged on a relatively strong footing from both the COVID-19 crisis and Russia's war in Ukraine. Real GDP grew by 2.5% in 2022, down from 4.5% the previous year, with the slowdown largely attributable to temporary disruptions to oil production. Kazakhstan's economic resilience in face of these shocks is testament to the sizeable buffers and prudent policy measures of the Kazakh authorities. Nevertheless, the growth outlook remains uncertain, with social unrest in January 2022, the continuation of Russia's war in Ukraine and the potential for further sanctions on Russia to affect Kazakhstan's trade, accelerating domestic inflation and tighter global financial conditions all contributing to a challenging short-to-medium term context.

While the country's resilience to recent shocks is positive, it is important that policymakers remain committed to implementing longer-term reforms to support private-sector development and greater diversification. Addressing the issues that prevent private firms from investing, hiring, innovating and growing will be key to improving the resilience of Kazakhstan in a global context that is rapidly becoming more digital and less carbon intensive.

Using insights derived from a private sector survey of foreign firms in Kazakhstan, this report examines three key issues in the business climate that may stymie the contribution and growth of the private sector in the country. Bringing together recent and new analysis of key policy areas for a vibrant business climate in the country, the report will be of use to local policymakers, international development partners, and other stakeholders interested in developing a diversified and resilient private sector in Kazakhstan.

Acknowledgements

This report was prepared by the OECD Eurasia Division of the OECD Global Relations and Co-operation Secretariat (GRC), under the guidance of Mr William Tompson, Head of the OECD Eurasia Division, and Mr Grégory Lecomte, Head of the Central Asia Unit. The work was carried out in the context of the OECD Eurasia Competitiveness Programme as part of the OECD Central Asia Initiative. The work was financed by the European Union (EU).

The report was drafted by Mr Luke Mackle, Policy Analyst at the OECD Eurasia Division. The report benefited from substantial statistical and editorial support from Mr Hugo Brisebard, Junior Policy Analyst at the OECD Eurasia Division. The report was enriched with substantive comments from Ms Peline Atamer, Programme Manager, and Ms Amélie Schurich-Rey and Ms Céléste Laporte, Policy Analysts, all of the OECD Eurasia Division. Valuable editorial and publication support was also provided by Ms Elisa Larrakoetxea, and excellent administrative support was provided by Ms Anna Chahtahtinsky, both of the OECD Eurasia Division.

The report draws upon a survey of private firms and private sector organisations in Kazakhstan, and the OECD is indebted to each of the firms and organisations that took the time to respond to the survey. The OECD is also grateful to a number of development partners that provided comments and reflections on the survey and its findings.

The OECD would like to thank colleagues at the Delegation of the European Delegation to Kazakhstan for their support in delivering this report. In particular, the OECD would like to thank Mr Kestutis Jankauska, Ambassador of the European Union (EU) to the Republic of Kazakhstan, Mr Johannes Baur, Head of Co-operation and Mr Youri Skaskevich, Attaché and Programme Officer, both at the EU Delegation to the Republic of Kazakhstan. The OECD would also like to thank Ms Sarah Rinaldi, Head of Unit of the Directorate-General of International Partnerships at the European Commission for her support.

Table of contents

FIGURES

TABLES

Executive summary

The key to Kazakhstan's economic development and resilience lies in the development of a robust and diversified private sector

Kazakhstan is the largest economy in Central Asia and a key hub for regional trade and investment. Since emerging from the transition recession in 1996, Kazakhstan has experienced real GDP growth of 5% per annum, while labour productivity and investment have also grown substantially, particularly in the first decade of the 2000s. The main driver of the country's strong economic performance has been and remains the extraction and export of its vast natural resources. Kazakhstan's economy is also highly internationalised, and it has been the country's openness to foreign investment and technology, as well as its engagement with the international trade architecture through institutions like the World Trade Organisation (WTO), that has allowed it to develop sophisticated industries so quickly in these sectors.

Nevertheless, Kazakhstan's socio-economic resilience is challenged by limited private-sector development. Extractives-fuelled growth has led to a concentration of economic output that is non-inclusive and vulnerable to external shocks. Extractives-driven growth has failed to drive the development of a private, dynamic non-resource tradable sector – and may in some respects have impeded it. Investment and the most productive jobs are concentrated in a handful of sectors that generate relatively little employment, in which SMEs play only a minor role, and which are vulnerable to changes in global demand for hydrocarbons. In the longer-term, the global push for net zero emissions, to which Kazakhstan is committed, may drastically reduce the competitiveness of the country's main growth drivers.

The key to further socio-economic development and resilience lies in the development of a robust and diversified private sector. To achieve this, the government must address the policy issues that have hitherto stymied private sector development, while also looking forward to the changing needs of firms in a rapidly transforming global context.

A 2022 survey of foreign firms in Kazakhstan highlighted opportunities and challenges for doing business in the country

The OECD surveyed a selection of foreign-owned private firms in Kazakhstan to gauge business sentiment with respect to the government's ongoing reform process and to help identify opportunities and challenges in the business climate. The survey was small but focussed, targeting European firms active in Kazakhstan, as well as a number of business and trade organisations. Respondents were asked to highlight reform progress and challenges, to highlight policy issues they considered priorities for action, to give their views on the impact of Russia's war in Ukraine and the global pandemic on doing business in Kazakhstan, and to share their thoughts on government policies to support the private sector in the context of the digital and green transitions.

Three overarching conclusions emerge from survey responses. They largely dovetail with prior OECD assessments of the business climate in Kazakhstan. First, firms noted that while the government has made significant progress in digitalising public service delivery, private sector digitalisation remains hampered by underinvestment in infrastructure and skills. Secondly, respondents praised government efforts to simplify the operational environment for firms, particularly the simplification of licensing and permitting processes, but also highlighted lingering issues around trade facilitation and contract enforcement. Thirdly, firms agreed that Kazakhstan had significantly increased the statutory openness of the economy but nevertheless highlighted challenges linked to competition and transparency that may act as *de facto* barriers to investment.

Improving connectivity infrastructure and skills could accelerate private-sector digitalisation

Survey respondents underscored their enthusiasm for digital opportunities in Kazakhstan. Some 80% reported that digitalisation was creating new opportunities for them in the country, and a significant majority of them reported that they already were using advanced digital tools. Firms were also positive on the use of digitalisation to improve public service delivery, lowering the time and cost involved for firms in interacting with public bodies. However, firms also noted that infrastructure and skills shortages were holding back the digital transformation.

There is a need for greater investment in the connectivity and digital infrastructure necessary for the digital transformation, as well as a regulatory environment that can support the digital transition. Kazakhstan has made significant progress providing firms and citizens with affordable access to broadband infrastructure, but challenges remain in improving the quality of that infrastructure. Regulatory issues may also slow the digital transition, for example through the impact of competition-related challenges on investment in the highly regulated telecommunications sector. A related issue is the low level of investment in information and communication technologies, which accounted for only 1.98% of total investment in 2019, significantly below the OECD average of 11.4%.

Better trade facilitation and contract enforcement will support diversification

Survey respondents were largely positive about the progress of numerous reforms to improve the operational environment for firms. Respondents overwhelmingly reported that many aspects of the regulatory and policy environment were conducive to doing business, with only 6% of respondents reporting that the business environment overall was unfriendly. Firms were positive about progress in a number of areas that affected day-to-day operations, particularly the simplification of registration and licensing requirements. A large majority also felt that the government had made progress over the past five years in implementing reforms to support the private sector.

Trade facilitation and contract enforcement nevertheless emerged as challenges for firms, which may have consequences for their ability to contribute to the government's diversification agenda. Kazakhstan has long recognised the importance of reforms to support trade facilitation, making it easier for local SMEs to trade internationally and compete abroad. While the country's performance in the OECD Trade Facilitation Indicators (TFIs) suggests that Kazakhstan has made progress in improving its trade facilitation framework, there remains a significant gap with the OECD average which targeted policy action could help narrow. A majority of firms also noted the importance of reforms to support contract enforcement. While Kazakhstan now has a clear legal framework for contract enforcement and dispute resolution, alleviating firms' concerns about the reliability of implementation and the transparency of decisions will be important for the government's ability to attract high-quality investment.

Reducing regulatory and competition-related barriers to investment could boost FDI

Policies to support foreign investors were among the most positively assessed by survey respondents. Flagship projects such as the Astana International Financial Centre and the creation of special economic zones were among the top three policies rated as very useful by respondents, whilst a plurality of respondents were also positive about the establishment of public private dialogue platforms such as the Foreign Investors' Council. This positive assessment of investor-related reforms comes in the context of a relatively open statutory regime for FDI, as reflected in Kazakhstan's good performance in the OECD FDI Regulatory Restrictiveness Index. Given the importance the government attaches to its investment attraction agenda, it is encouraging that a number of its interventions have been well received by those investors already operating in the country.

Nevertheless, actual levels of foreign investment remain low, particularly outside the primary sector. If the overall statutory regime for FDI is relatively open, there are nevertheless a number of regulatory restrictions – particularly in services trade, but also in certain network sectors – that may impede investment. Similarly, whilst the government is pushing ahead with pro-competition reform agenda, challenges with the implementation of policies to support the development of a level playing field between public and private firms may act as *de facto* barriers for both domestic and foreign investors.

Addressing the challenges highlighted in the report can help Kazakhstan sustain strong, inclusive growth

Kazakhstan has the potential to sustain strong growth over the longer term, but achieving this end will require further structural reforms to facilitate structural transformation and the shift to a more sustainable, diversified and inclusive growth model. There are both daunting challenges and enormous opportunities ahead, particularly those linked to the green and digital transitions. The authorities have committed themselves to a wide range of needed structural reforms – not only those addressed by the present survey – and also to continued macroeconomic discipline. Implementing many of these reforms is likely to prove far more difficult than designing and adopting them, however, and will place great demands on the political will and administrative capacities of the state. If the government is able to deliver on its reform commitments, it can lay the foundations for a better future for its citizens.

1 Introduction

The private sector survey that formed the starting point of this report allowed the OECD to identify three key issues facing firms in Kazakhstan. Whilst progress has been made in many areas of the business climate, firms continue to face challenges with digital infrastructure and skills, operational aspects of the business environment such as trade facilitation and contract enforcement, and regulatory restrictions on investment in certain areas of the economy. This chapter introduces the context for the survey and the high-level insights that emerge from it.

1.1. Introduction

Kazakhstan is the largest economy in Central Asia. Since independence, economic growth has been primarily fuelled by the extraction and export of a narrow range of commodities – principally hydrocarbons and other minerals – that the country has in abundance. The country's extractive sectors remain crucial to growth and a key driver of investment. Nevertheless, these sectors contribute relatively little in terms of direct job creation and the rents they have generated are concentrated among a few, primarily state-owned, firms. These sectors will remain economically important in the years ahead, but their ability to form the cornerstone of a sustainable and inclusive model of growth has proven limited.

Kazakhstan emerged on a relatively strong footing following the COVID-19 crisis, and as of spring 2023 the impact of Russia's war in Ukraine has been muted. The economy grew by 2.5% in 2022, down from 4.3% the previous year, with the slowdown largely attributable to temporary disruptions to oil production. The ability of the country to weather recent economic shocks is testament both to the sizeable buffers and prudent policy measures of the Kazakh authorities, as well as the agility with which they responded to business and societal needs during a period of significant disruption. Nevertheless, the growth outlook is uncertain, with social unrest in January 2022, the continuation of Russia's war in Ukraine and the potential for further sanctions on Russia to affect Kazakhstan's trade, accelerating domestic inflation and tighter global financial conditions all contributing to a challenging short-to-medium term context.

The resilience of Kazakhstan's economy continues to be hampered by a relatively underdeveloped private sector (World Bank, 2021[1]). Addressing the issues that prevent the private sector from investing, hiring, and growing will be key to improving the resilience of the country in the years ahead. It will also be key to the success of Kazakhstan in navigating the twin transitions of digitalisation and decarbonisation. This report presents a number of insights on key business climate issues that have been drawn from a survey of foreign firms active in Kazakhstan. Using recent OECD analysis on these selected issues, the report aims to support policy makers in Kazakhstan to effectively the most pressing questions facing the business community in the country.

1.1.1. The unrealised potential of private sector development in Kazakhstan

Private sector development is a long-standing, but only partially fulfilled ambition of successive governments in Kazakhstan. Despite being a major component of socio-economic development documents and plans such as the "100 Concrete Steps" programme and the "Kazakhstan 2050 Strategy", the significant potential of the non-oil private sector remains unrealised. While there has been a notable growth in services since independence and their concomitant contribution to growth and employment, many service sector firms and jobs are in non-tradable activities such as construction and retail, which are characterised by low productivity and where business is linked to the redistribution – often from the state – of revenues from the extractive sector.

The government has made significant progress in lowering the cost of doing business, and Kazakhstan is now significantly more business friendly than in the past (EBRD, 2019[2]). In recent years, reforms to simplify business registration and licensing, the introduction of new, clearer business legislation, reforms to the tax code and investment regulation, the development of special economic zones and new institutions for domestic capital markets are among the many ways in which the authorities have made Kazakhstan an increasingly business-friendly location. Much of this has been supported by concerted effort to use digital tools to improve government service delivery and increase transparency, with government digitalisation being an area where Kazakhstan has made significant advances. In 2019, for instance, obtaining an electrical connection was twice as fast in Kazakhstan than in Europe and Central Asia, thus testifying to efficient access to physical infrastructure that represents a major cost of doing business. Similarly, the obtention of permits and licenses was faster in the country that in Europe or Central Asia.

Nevertheless, that the private sector remains relatively underdeveloped is reflective of a number of prevailing weaknesses in the business climate (IMF, 2021[3]). The development of private enterprise remains impeded by a number of policy and governance issues. Many of these relate to the role of the state in the economy, issues around competition and the speed of pro-market reforms, access to finance, corruption, infrastructure, and skills. In numerous areas, the significant *de jure* improvement to the business environment has not been accompanied by reliable implementation.

What constitutes a strong "business climate" is in reality a complex interconnection of numerous different policy areas. Responsibility for the design and implementation of these different areas, as well as defining the rationale for intervention in different areas, is therefore spread across a large number of government institutions and bodies. One of the major challenges for Kazakhstan is therefore ensuring that those responsible for these various policy areas – competition, fiscal, investment, education, environment, labour – are well coordinated and aligned. Weaknesses in one, such as competition, can undermine the most determined of efforts in others.

1.1.2. The push for net zero: an addition rationale for diversification

The extractive sectors of Kazakhstan's economy remain vital for the government's revenue base and sustaining the fiscal buffers that shielded the country from the worst of the COVID shock. Nevertheless, as a model for long-term economic development, such heavy reliance on extractive sectors is fundamentally fragile and unsustainable. Global commodity price fluctuations make Kazakhstan's economy vulnerable to external shocks, typified by the 2008-09 global financial crisis and its impact on international oil demand, the 2014-15 commodity price crash, and more recently the disruptive – with variegated impact channels – experience of the COVID-19 pandemic and Russia's war of aggression in Ukraine on global production, demand, and supply chains.

Diminishing returns to growth from the extractive sector in a global context of decarbonisation redoubles the importance of diversification. The ability of Kazakhstan's extractive sectors to fuel growth is diminishing. Resource extraction as a driver of growth has begun to run out of steam. In the longer-term, and perhaps of greater significance, the global sustainability transition will erode the competitiveness of Kazakhstan's major industries. The international push towards net zero emissions codified in the Paris Agreement on Climate – to which Kazakhstan is a signatory, and committed to achieving carbon neutrality by 2060 – may make many of the country's key drivers of growth obsolete or untenable in the longer term.

The global push for more sustainable and less carbon intensive modes of economic production and organisation is changing what government and society expect from private enterprise. No longer does the rationale for policy support stop at job creation and productivity; firms must also become engines of the sustainability transition, investing in the technologies, knowledge and infrastructure needed to address climate challenges.

1.1.3. Drawing on a private sector survey, this report presents areas for policy action

The content of the report is guided by a survey of international – primarily European – firms operating in Kazakhstan. The survey was an opportunity to gauge business sentiment among a small cohort of international firms of the type that the government is actively seeking to attract to the country. The concerns, observations and positive appraisals gathered through the survey largely dovetail with the OECD's own analysis on business climate issues in Kazakhstan.

The survey was small but focused. It targeted 27 foreign firms active in Kazakhstan, the majority of which are entirely or partly owned by entities based in the European Union, as well as four foreign chambers of commerce or trade representation offices. The survey presented an opportunity to gather bottom-up, firm-level perceptions on policy issues relating to the business climate and private-sector development in Kazakhstan. The survey insights are largely congruent with previous OECD work on business climate issues in Kazakhstan and reinforce the need for policy change. The report sheds light on three issues that were raised by survey respondents:

1. **Kazakhstan has made significant progress in digitalising public service delivery and the public sector more broadly, but the extent of digital uptake in the private sector remains low.** Ensuring that firms have the infrastructure and skills necessary to take advantage of the digital transformation is crucial to their long-term competitiveness. Significant progress is needed to provide the private sector with the quality digital and connectivity infrastructure and skills that firms need to make the most of digitalisation.
2. **The government has markedly lowered the fixed costs of doing business through regulatory simplification and improvements to government services such as licensing and registration.** Nevertheless, there remains a significant number of challenges in the *de facto* operational environment for private firms, particularly with issues around trade facilitation and contract enforcement.
3. **There have been notable efforts to improve the investment attractiveness of Kazakhstan, but competition and transparency issues undermine efforts to bring new investment, particularly in non-extractive sectors.** That a number of the most pressing policy issues facing foreign investors and businesses are not issues of investment policy *per se*, but more structural matters of competition and transparency speak to the need for, *inter alia*, a more holistic, whole-of-government approach to supporting private sector development.

Taken together, these results provide important context for the OECD's ongoing work to support the improvement of the business climate in Kazakhstan and help to corroborate and validate the emphasis placed by the OECD on a number of priority areas for reform for the authorities. This includes the importance of improving both the hard and soft infrastructure needed for trade within Kazakhstan and with its regional neighbours; the importance of tackling inveterately difficult issues around competition and regulatory enforcement; and the importance of investments in the infrastructure and skills necessary to enable firms to not just be objects of the digital and green transitions, but to be active agents in these structural changes and to benefit from them.

Responses to the survey also suggest that firms are aware of the opportunities and challenges of the sustainability transition. A significant plurality report that they are actively adopting new technologies and operations to reduce their carbon footprints and support the government's stated climate change and sustainability ambitions. At the same time, **a majority of firms report that policy support for the green transition remains insufficient, and call for greater investment in sustainable infrastructure, better environmental standards, and stronger financial incentives for the adoption of greener practices within firms**.

1.1.4. The structure of the report

In Chapter 2, the report proceeds with an introduction to key aspects of the economic context for private sector development in Kazakhstan. The chapter introduces recent trends in growth, investment, trade and productivity, while also giving an overview of the broader progress with important aspects of the government's policy agenda, notably in diversification. Chapter 3 then introduces the survey that informs the remainder of the report. The final three chapters of the report each pick up and expand upon the three policy areas issues that outlined above.

Chapter 4 begins with an overview of private sector digitalisation, building upon firm responses that called for further development of the digital and connectivity infrastructure necessary for success in a digital context, and provides an overview of issues relating to digital skills. Chapter 5 expands upon two issues in the operational environment that were highlighted by firms in the survey: policies to support trade facilitation, and contract enforcement. This chapter introduces insights from the OECD Trade Facilitation indicators and draws upon recent OECD work on the legal environment for business in Kazakhstan. Chapter 6 concludes the report with an overview of recent reforms to support foreign direct investment in Kazakhstan and highlights a number of areas where regulatory and competition barriers may still act as impediments to achieving the government's agenda of attracting higher levels of quality foreign direct investment.

References

EBRD (2019), *Enteprise Surveys: Kazakhstan 2019 Country Profile*, EBRD/World Bank Group, https://www.enterprisesurveys.org/content/dam/enterprisesurveys/documents/country-profiles/Kazakhstan-2019.pdf. [2]

EBRD (2017), *Kazakhstan diagnostic paper: Assessing progress and challenges in developing a sustainable market economy*, EBRD, https://www.ebrd.com/publications/country-diagnostics. [8]

IMF (2021), *Kazakhstan Staff Concluding Statement of the 2021 Article IV Mission*, https://www.imf.org/en/News/Articles/2021/11/17/kazakhstan-staff-concluding-statement-of-the-2021-article-iv-mission (accessed on 18 May 2022). [3]

OECD (2022), *Weathering Economic Storms in Central Asia*, OECD Publishing, https://www.oecd.org/publications/weathering-economic-storms-in-central-asia-83348924-en.htm. [4]

OECD (2021), *Beyond COVID-19: Prospects for Economic Recovery in Central Asia*, OECD Publishing, Paris, https://www.oecd.org/eurasia/Beyond_COVID%2019_Central%20Asia.pdf. [5]

OECD (2021), *Improving the Legal Environment for Business and Investment in Central Asia*, OECD Publishing, Paris, https://www.oecd.org/eurasia/Improving-LEB-CA-ENG%2020%20April.pdf. [6]

World Bank (2021), *Economic Recovery During Challenging Times: Kazakhstan Economic Update Winter 2021/2022*, World Bank, DC, https://documents1.worldbank.org/curated/en/566741640158785669/pdf/Kazakhstan-Economic-Update-Economic-Recovery-during-Challenging-Times.pdf. [1]

World Bank (2018), *Kazakhstan - Systemtic Country Diagnostic: A New Growth Model for Building a Secure Middle Class*, World Bank, DC, http://documents.worldbank.org/curated/en/801771549867544115/Kazakhstan-Systematic-Country-Diagnostic-A-New-Growth-Model-for-Building-a-Secure-Middle-Class. [7]

2 An economic overview of Kazakhstan: trends and challenges

Despite undergoing significant structural transformation since 1991, the resilience and competitiveness of Kazakhstan's economy remains challenged by limited private-sector development and a high degree of economic concentration in the country's extractive sectors. While many macroeconomic trends are doubtlessly strong, the benefits of the country's extractive-fuelled growth have not been sufficiently shared throughout the economy, resulting in uneven productivity growth, investment and inclusion. This chapter introduces some of the key economic trends and challenges in Kazakhstan that are relevant to contextualise this survey and the policy specific chapters later in the report.

2.1. Overview and policy context

More than three decades since Kazakhstan became independent, reducing the role of the state in the economy, developing the private-sector and fostering economic diversification remain important priorities for the government. To achieve these ends, the government has developed numerous economic development strategies, invested significant public resources in industrialisation programmes, and implemented a range of regulatory and legal reforms to support domestic and international business. The impact of these policy interventions has been varied. Kazakhstan has undoubtedly become a much easier and more attractive country for doing business, and the country's macroeconomic performance over the past two decades has been impressive (OECD, 2021[1]). At the same time, progress in transforming the role of the state in the economy from the primary driver of economic output to a facilitator of private-sector growth, and in diversifying and increasing the resilience of the economy, remains limited.

Kazakhstan has significantly deepened its co-operation with the OECD in recent years. The country is an active member in a number of substantive committees and working groups, and there is regular work and co-operation between the OECD and the government of Kazakhstan on identifying and implementing reforms to support its journey towards OECD standards. Domestically, the government's guiding strategies for economic reform, such as the "Kazakhstan-2050" programme and the Strategic Development Plan 2025, prioritise a number of areas where progress could directly address issues highlighted in the report as well as in the broader body of OECD work on Kazakhstan.

This chapter is structured around a number of observations on Kazakhstan's economy that are relevant to the report and ongoing policy debates to support private-sector development in the country. Section 2.2 introduces some high-level socio-economic trends that give context to the broader discussions in the report. Section 2.3 gives an overview of questions of structural transformation and diversification, while Section 2.4 discusses private-sector development and business dynamism. Section 2.5 concludes with an overview of the country's external trade position and integration into global value chains (GVCs).

2.2. Disruption and resilience: key socio-economic trends

Kazakhstan has made significant progress since beginning its transition to a market economy in 1991. After emerging from the post-transition recession in 1996, Kazakhstan's real GDP has grown at an average annual rate of 5.0%, in line with the regional average of 5.4%, and above the OECD average of 2% over the same period (Figure 2.1) (World Bank, 2023[2]).[1] FDI stocks in the last pre-pandemic year of 2019 equalled 84.0% GDP, a 28.9 pp increase since 2000, while net inflows were equal to 2.1% GDP, down from 7.5% over the same period as above (UNCTAD, 2023[3]) (World Bank, 2023[2]). Part of the drop-off in inflows can be explained by that FDI in countries with capital-intensive extractive sectors can be irregular but substantial when it occurs, whilst the volume of both inflows and stocks relative to GDP, which has grown substantially since 2000, obscures the fact that both measurements nevertheless demonstrate a significant expansion of inward investment in nominal terms.

Figure 2.1. Real GDP growth in Central Asia (2010-2022)

Growth in Kazakhstan has been decelerating over the past decade

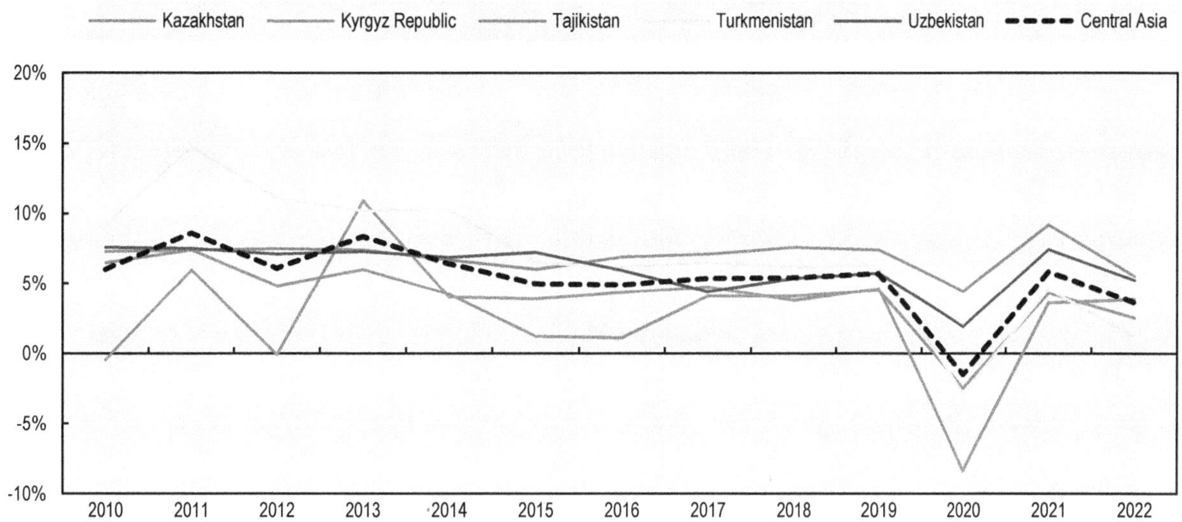

Source: (World Bank, 2023[2])

From 2010 to 2021, labour productivity increased by 35%, measured in terms of value added per worker, while levels of poverty have fallen by 32% since 2000 (measured as the percentage of population living on below USD 6.85 PPP per day). Since 2015, the unemployment rate has consistently remained around 4.9%, against a Central Asian average of 5.2%, while youth (15-24 years old) unemployment, at 4% in 2021, is below the regional average of 10.7%. Total external debt reached 83.6% GDP in 2021, with gross public debt at 25.1% GDP in the same year (IMF, 2022[4]).

GDP and productivity growth are decelerating. Although GDP growth remains stronger than in most OECD economies, it has been decelerating since 2001, with the deceleration intensifying following the Global Financial Crisis of 2008-09 (GFC) and the 2014-15 commodity price shock. Having steadily converged with the OECD average from around 2000, the convergence process began to stagnate following the 2014-15 commodity crash (Figure 2.2a). A similar trend is true of productivity growth, which has slowed in recently years, particularly after the GFC, and which remains around 60% of the OECD average (Figure 2.2b). The productivity slowdown has been more pronounced in non-extractive sectors, which continue to account for the largest share of employment but lower shares of domestic and foreign investment. At the firm level, the productivity of SMEs is roughly half that of larger firms in the country, the latter predominating in the country's extractive sectors, indicating that aggregate levels of productivity growth mask an uneven distribution of this growth across the private-sector (EBRD, 2017[5]) (EBRD, 2022[6]).

Figure 2.2. Growth in Kazakhstan: regional context, OECD convergence, the resource question, and contributions

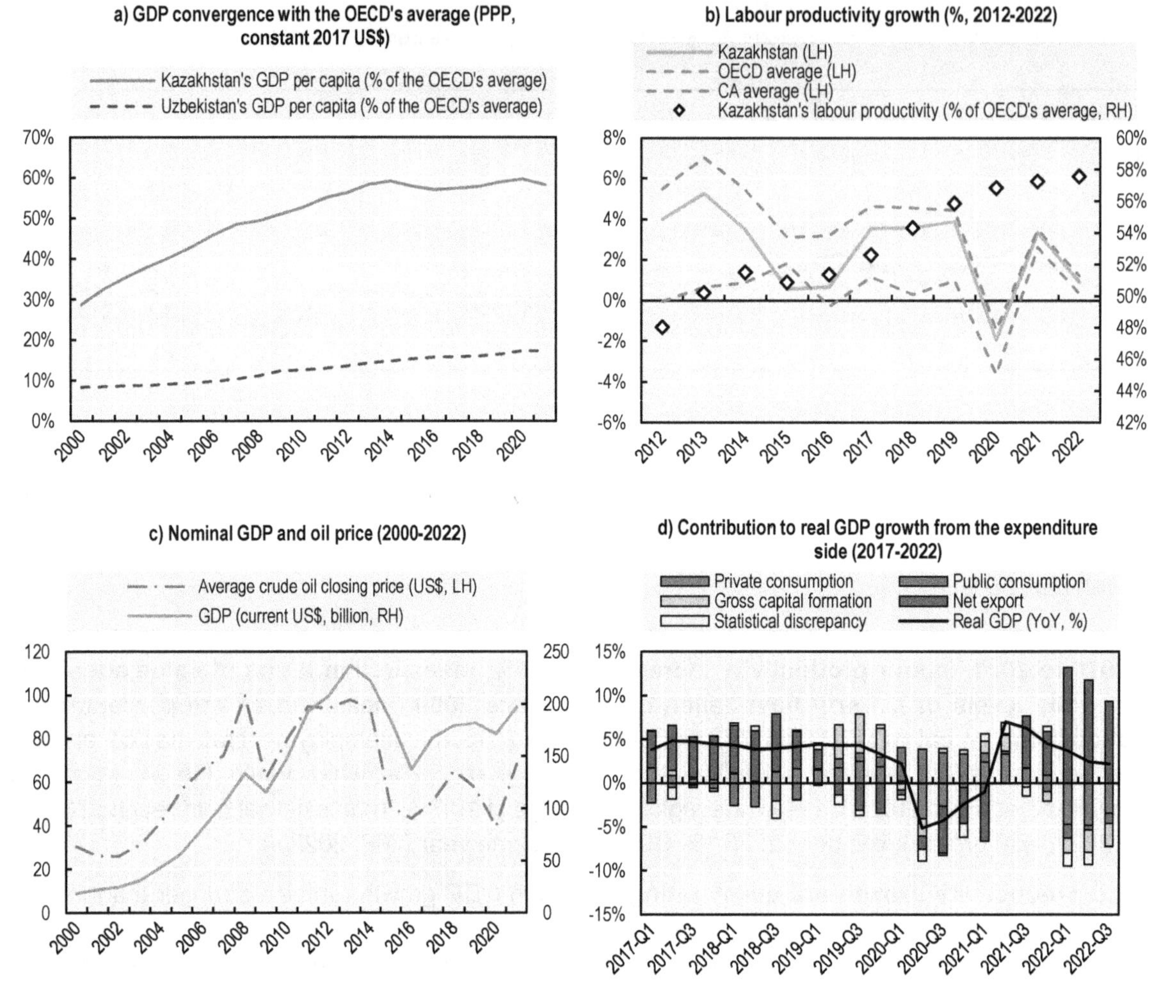

Note: OECD calculations based on OECD data and data from the National Statistics Office of Kazakhstan; Uzbekistan included as a comparator in charts throughout this report due to its inclusion in an accompanying report.
Source: (MacroTrends, 2023[7]) (World Bank, 2023[2]) (National Statistics Office of Kazakhstan, 2023[8]) (ILO, 2023[9])

Growth continues to be primarily driven by the extraction and export of natural resources. For over two decades, Kazakhstan's growth has been closely correlated to global oil prices (Figure 2.2 c); as the price of oil has risen, so too has GDP, with the reverse also true. This reflects the fact that net exports – the majority of which are hydrocarbons – are one of the key contributors to annual growth (Figure 2.2 d). Particularly high prices for oil have helped offset significant public spending during the global pandemic, with a 70% growth of government revenues in 2022 largely attributable to the international price of oil (2021-2022 seeing a 177% increase in oil revenues vs. 27% for non-oil revenues, with only a modest increase in export volumes) (IMF, 2022[4]).

The extractive sector therefore continues to be a major source not just of growth, but of fiscal resilience, enabling the government to accumulate significant buffers. One major challenge for the government is dealing with the volatility that an overreliance on resource rents creates for macroeconomic stability (for example, via exchange rate volatility), and the concomitant challenges of developing a sound and predictable environment for business. At the same time, the government must contend with the fact that, whilst it remains a competitive exporter of hydrocarbons, the global decarbonisation transition will erode this competitiveness; the IEA expects, if signatories to the Paris Agreement on Climate meet their stated net zero targets, that global demand for hydrocarbons will fall 50% by 2050 (IEA, 2022[10]).

Although Kazakhstan has one of the most energy-intensive economies in the world, the country is increasing the productivity of emissions and energy consumption relative to output. Kazakhstan's CO2 intensity – the volume of CO2 required to produce 1 USD PPP of output – fell almost by 50% between 2000 and 2020, although current levels (0.45kg CO2/USD PPP) remain 73% above the global average (Figure 2.3a) (IEA, 2022[11]). At the same time, the energy productivity of growth is improving (calculated as GDP per unit of total energy supply, expressed as the ratio of USD/tonne of oil equivalent). In 2000, 1 tonne of oil equivalent (TOE) in Kazakhstan would have produced USD 4,098 in output, compared to USD 6,925 in output in 2020. This represents a significant increase in the productivity energy in growth, but it is nevertheless a level that remains far below the OECD average, where the equivalent TOE would produce 1.6 times as much economic output (Figure 2.3b).

Figure 2.3. CO2 and energy intensity of Kazakhstan's economy

Output has become more energy efficient and less carbon intensive, but Kazakhstan remains far more energy and emission intensive than the OECD average

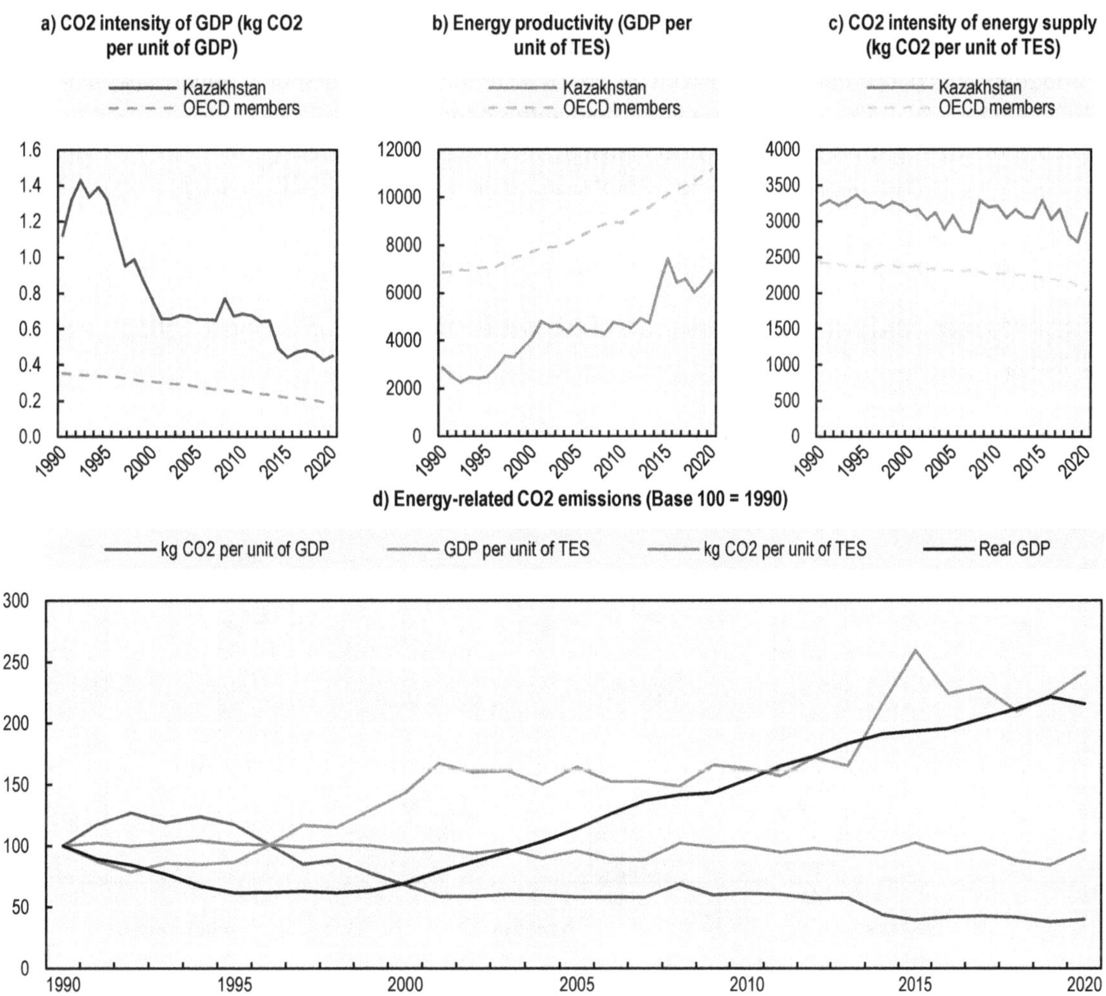

Note: GDP is expressed in USD, 2015.
Source: (OECD, 2023[12])

The persistently high levels of CO2 emissions and energy required for Kazakhstan's growth is due to the carbon footprint of the extractive sector, and the dominance of fossil fuels in the country's energy supply. Nevertheless, there is a positive downwards trend across most emissions intensity and growth indicators, including the CO2 intensity per unit of total energy supply (a key factor in the decarbonisation of the domestic energy sector), which indicates that Kazakhstan is gradually modernising its industrial base and the energy sector (Figure 2.3c). Bringing Kazakhstan closer to OECD standards in terms of energy and CO2 intensity, and therefore closer to the government's own long-term emissions reduction targets, will require significant investment in infrastructure.

There is a significant public health cost to the emissions-intensive nature of Kazakhstan's economy. The OECD estimates that Kazakhstan has a significant level of premature deaths due to particulate matter (PM2.5) exposure (slightly below 600 per 1,000,000 inhabitants), and that the welfare costs of premature mortality due to exposure to PM2.5 pollution amount to around 6% GDP in 2019 (OECD, 2022[13]). In part, this reflects the fact that some 98.6% of Kazakhstan's population are exposed to PM2.5 in the air, a level which is not only substantially higher than the OECD average of 61.6%, but which has remained stubbornly flat since 2000, whilst the corresponding level in the OECD has gradually fallen over the same period (OECD, 2023[14]).

2.3. Structural change and diversification

Kazakhstan experienced a rapid process of structural transformation in the 1990s. Since 1992, the value added of agriculture has dropped from 23.2% of GDP to 5%, a level that is nevertheless higher than the OECD average of 1.4%. At the same time, the value added of the services sector jumped from 25.1% around 55% of GDP, a level that is also significantly below the OECD average of 71%. The value added of manufacturing fell steadily, from 16% to 13%of GDP, in line with the OECD average (Figure 2.4).

Figure 2.4. Value added of the agricultural, manufacturing and service sectors (% GDP)

Kazakhstan has seen significant growth in the share of services in value added, with drops in agriculture and manufacturing

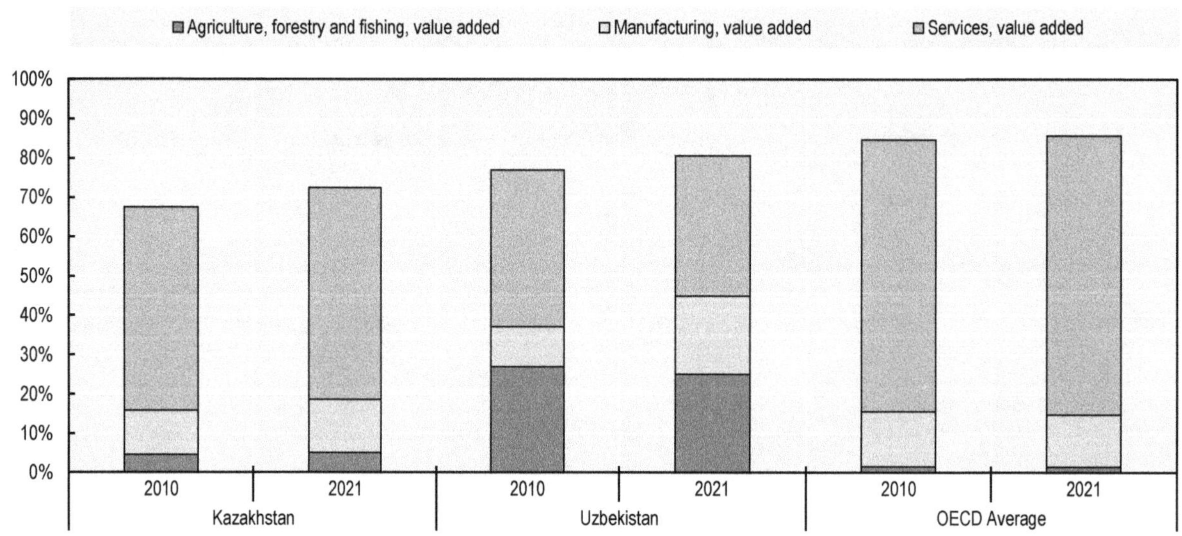

Note: Value added by industries in current USD prices
Source: (UN, 2023[15]) (World Bank, 2023[2])

The economic logic of structural change is the reallocation of labour and capital to lower productive activities to higher ones, yet many people in Kazakhstan employed in low productivity jobs. Some 81.5% of the population are employed in sectors where productivity is around or below the national average (Figure 2.5), though the high degree of economic informality – particularly in low productivity sectors such as trade and agriculture – may mean that there are in fact more workers in lower productivity activities than official data suggest. One of the challenges for Kazakhstan is that the national average is 28% of the average of the three most productive sectors – mining, real estate services, and manufacturing. As a consequence, there emerges a significant issue around the inclusivity of growth, since these most productive sectors account for the most productive jobs and highest levels of investment but contribute little to overall employment (a combined 11.7%). What is more, the sustainability of these sectors is highly uncertain, both in terms of their vulnerability to short-term price shocks and their exposure to the longer-term effects of global decarbonisation. The productivity picture that emerges at a national level therefore masks significant sustainability and inclusion challenges, be it at the sectoral, firm, gender or regional level.

Around 41% of the population are employed in sectors where average productivity is less than half of the national average. For example, the education sector accounts for 12.7% employment and the public administration 5.5%, but the value added per worker in these sectors is 2.9 million KZT and 3.2 million KZT respectively, significantly below the national average of 9 million KZT. The agricultural sector continues to account for 13.4% of total employment, with value added per worker averaging KZT 3.6 million (around USD 7,750). The challenge for policymakers is ensuring that the benefits of strong macroeconomic performance are distributed throughout society in a way which is inclusive and underpins social cohesion.

Figure 2.5. Value added per worker and sectoral share of employment, 2021

High-productivity sectors account for a small share of total employment

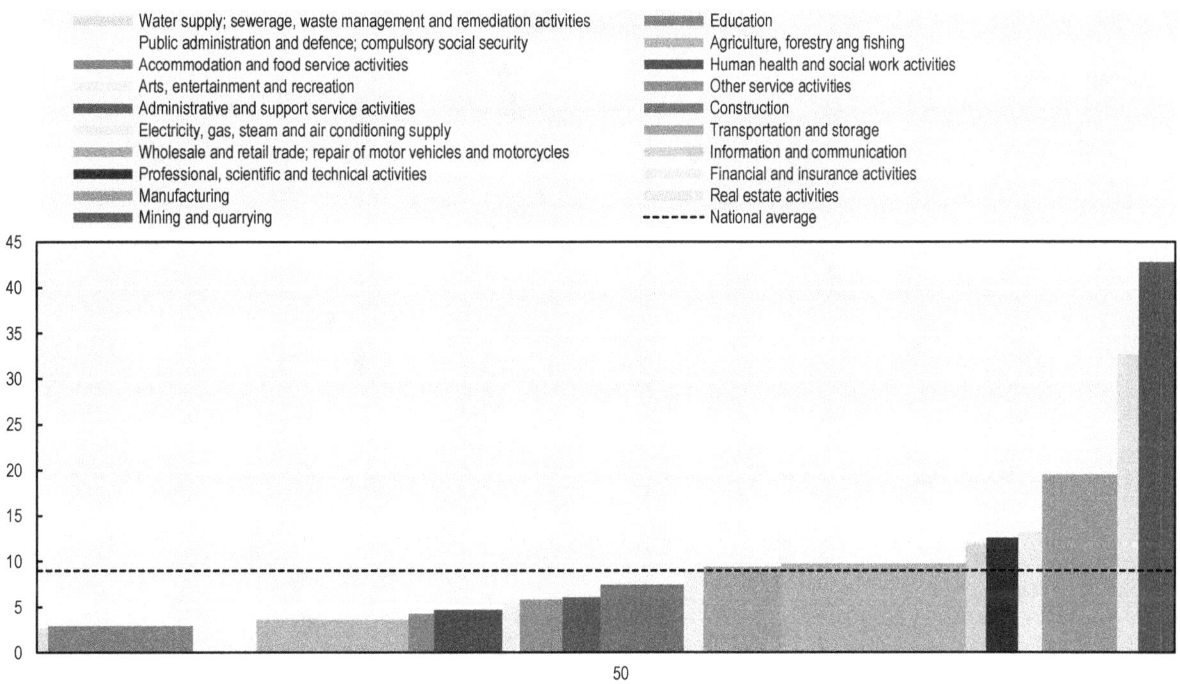

Note: Horizontal axis runs 0-100%. It is important to note that the chart does not show informal employment, which remains significant in Kazakhstan as in other countries in Central Asia.
Source: OECD calculations based (ILO, 2023[9]) and (UN, 2023[15])

The depth and resilience of structural change is linked to the more challenging issue of diversification. To a significant extent, the expansion of Kazakhstan's service sector – whether it is job creation in high-value services like finance or lower-value ones like retail and hospitality – has been driven by rents from the export of primary commodities. This is not to diminish successes in creating high-quality service sector jobs in Kazakhstan, but to highlight the link between diversification and the resilience of the non-tradable sector. Another of the major challenges for the government is to insulate the determinants of private-sector success – investment, productivity growth, innovation etc. – from the volatility of the terms of trade.

As noted in Section 2.2, a significant component of Kazakhstan's economic success is attributable to the hydrocarbon sector. In 2020, the fuel exports represented half of the value of Kazakhstan's total exports, with net exports one of the key contributors to GDP growth (Observatory of Economic Complexity, 2023[16]). Expanding the definition of the extractive sector to include fuels, material processing and crude materials would mean that the extractive sector accounted for 76% of total exports and 29% of GDP (OECD, 2020[17]). The challenge for Kazakhstan is that, as important economically as the extractive sector is, the extent of positive and durable linkages with the broader economy in terms of generating productivity and competitiveness is limited, and may even impede the ability of firms in non-oil sectors to grow and innovate via so-called "Dutch Disease" (Frankel and Romer, 1999[18]) (Corden and Neary, 1982[19]).

Kazakhstan has started to diversify its economy, but the impact on the composition of output has been limited. One of the clearest indications of the limited impact of diversification in Kazakhstan is the concentration of its export basket. Between 2000 and 2019, Kazakhstan significantly increased the range of products it exports, becoming by far the most diversified exporter in Central Asia in terms of the number of different export products and moving much closer to the OECD average (Figure 2.6) Yet the significant increase in the number of products exported has made only minimal difference to the concentration of the country's exports in volume terms.

Figure 2.6. Export diversification (2019)

Kazakhstan has increased the number of different products it exports, but the concentration of exports has nevertheless increased since 2000 in nominal and volume terms

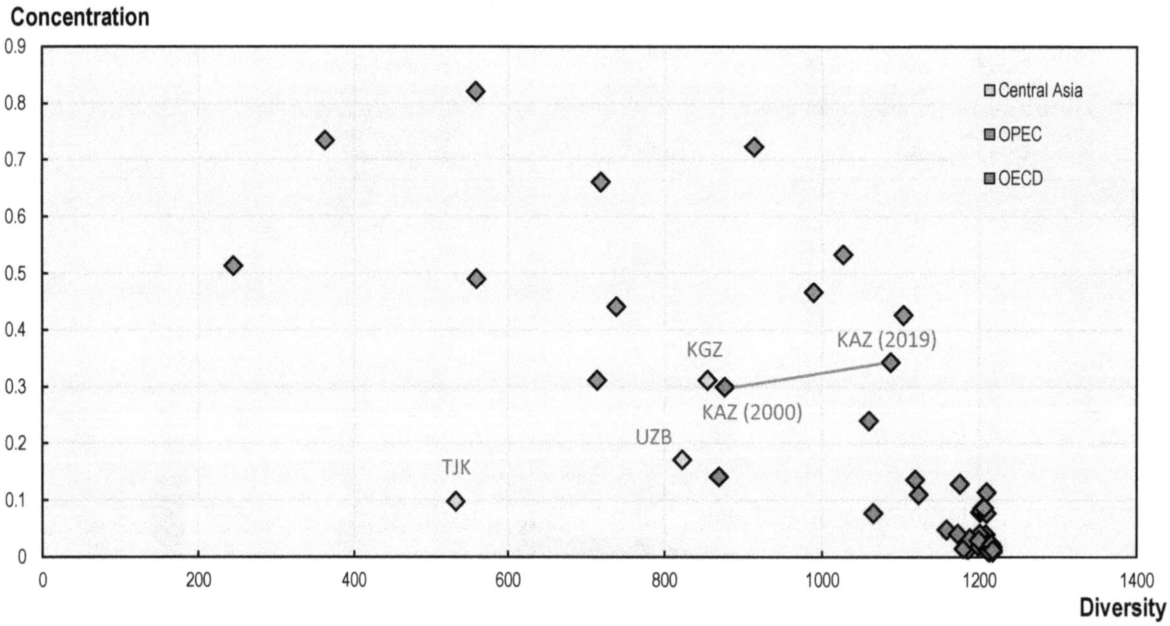

Note: Concentration of exports is measured with a normalized Herfindahl-Hirschman index (HHI) on exported products classified according to the HS 4-digits system. Diversity is measured as the number of exported products according to the HS 4-digits system. The HHI is an index traditionally used to assess the concentration of markets for competition regulators, with a value of 0.15 being competitive, 0.15-0.25 moderately concentrated, and above 0.25 being highly concentrated.
Source: OECD computation based on OEC data (Observatory of Economic Complexity, 2023[16])

In other words, despite exporting a wider range of products, the overall concentration of the country's export basket attributable to hydrocarbon products in terms of volume and value has in fact increased. The 0.3 HHI value of Kazakhstan's export basket in 2019 can be considered to be highly concentrated, similar to that of the 0.496 average of OPEC countries, and significantly higher than the OECD average of 0.042 and above the Central Asia average of 0.23, though this is nevertheless relatively concentrated. That the volume of non-oil exports remains low is indicative of the competitiveness and connectivity barriers SMEs in non-oil sectors face in international trade, which is discussed in Section 2.3 below; a more detailed breakdown of Kazakhstan's trade is given in Section 2.5.

2.4. Private-sector development and business dynamism

SMEs are a major driver of employment and growth, and their dynamism can be seen as a broader indicator of the health of the business climate. In 2022, small firms accounted for 97.7% of all firms in Kazakhstan, while medium-sized firms accounted for 1.6% and large firms 0.6%. As well as being the largest section of the business community, the weight of SMEs in Kazakhstan's economy has increased over the past two decades, with the share of SMEs in Kazakhstan's gross value added (GVA) rising from 6% of GDP in 2005 to 34% in 2021, with the share in employment increasing from 16% to 40% over the same period (Figure 2.7).

Figure 2.7. SME share in trade, GDP and employment (2005-2021)

The share of SMEs in employment and value-added has grown steadily since 2005

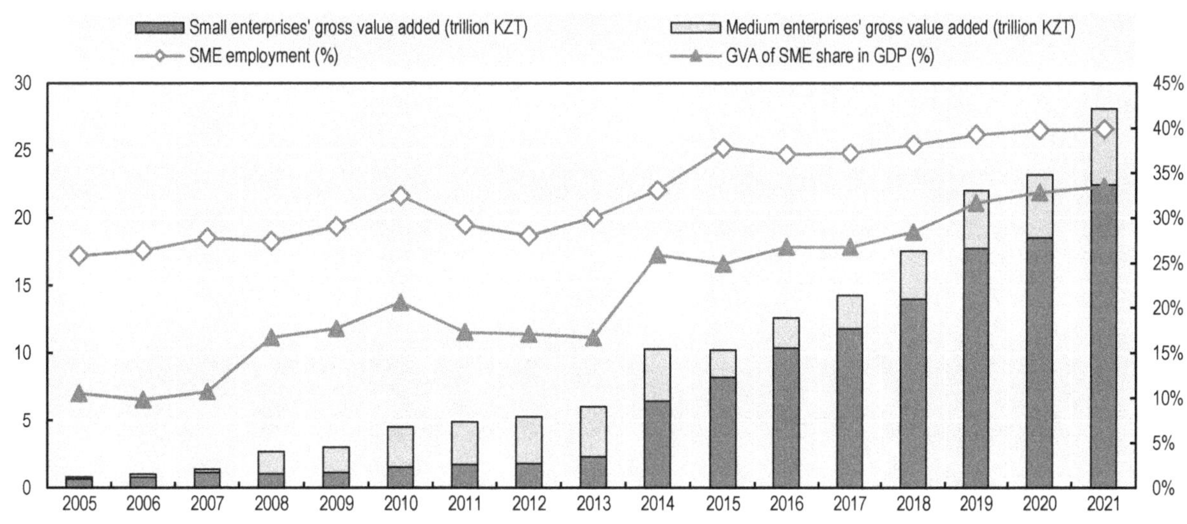

Note: GVA is expressed in trillion Tenge.
Source: OECD calculations based on data from National Statistics Office of Kazakhstan (National Statistics Office of Kazakhstan, 2023[20])

The contribution of SMEs to trade is growing, but firm internationalisation is held back by productivity and connectivity barriers. While the total number of SMEs has grown, firm growth has largely been in (often non-tradable) sectors with relatively low levels of internationalisation and productivity. While the lack of productivity in these sectors may be attributable to domestic business climate issues, the general competitiveness issue may be further compounded by the "Dutch Disease" of resource dependence, which via the channel of currency appreciation raises the relative cost of non-oil exports, thereby lowering their competitiveness on international markets. Lastly, Kazakhstan faces significant connectivity penalties. The country is large, geographically remote, and largely peripheral to global trade flows, and addressing these penalties requires significant investment in sustainable and high-quality connectivity infrastructure as well as considerable improvements to the country's soft infrastructure of customs and other trade-related regulation (ITF, 2019[21]).

Successive reforms to support private-sector development have made it easier to do business in Kazakhstan. The operational environment for opening and operating a business – in terms of the ease of registration, managing licensing and permitting etc. – has become significantly easier in recent years. It is perhaps unsurprising that, given the increased ease of doing business and relatively strong macroeconomic performance, there has been a significant increase in the number of new firms operating in Kazakhstan (Figure 2.8). Between 2010 and 2022, higher productivity sectors such as mining and manufacturing have seen significant increases in the number of firms operating (102% and 107% respectively), though the contribution of these firms to the overall business population (1% and 4.9%) and employment (3.2% and 6.6%) in 2022 was still relatively low. At the same time, some of the sharpest rates of firm growth were in lower productivity sectors such as agriculture (a 272% increase) and construction (205%).

Figure 2.8. Business dynamism in Kazakhstan (2010-2022)

There has been significant growth in the number of firms, particularly in non-tradable services

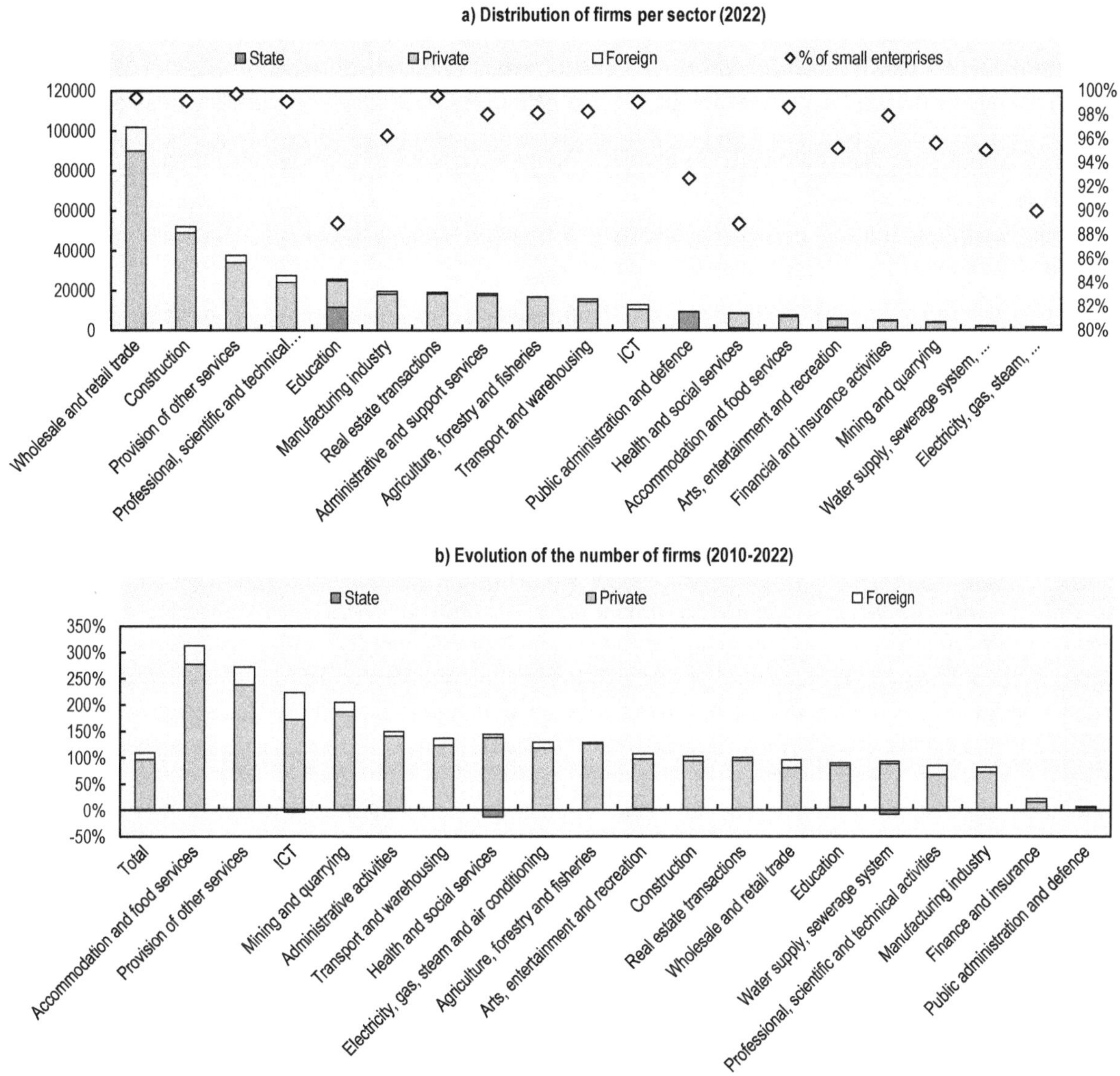

Source: OECD calculations based on enterprise data from the National Committee of Statistics of Kazakhstan

SMEs are present in most sectors of the economy. The largest number of SMEs are found in trade, construction and other undefined services. The sectors the fewest SMEs are education, healthcare, and electricity provision, though this in large part reflects the role of large SOEs in these areas of the economy. It is unsurprising that the footprint of SMEs is smaller in the extractive sectors and sectors adjacent to them (such as manufacturing), but there are nevertheless a large number of smaller enterprises in the industrial ecosystems and supply chains of these higher productivity areas. There has also been a notable growth in the number of foreign firms operating in Kazakhstan. The number of firms with foreign ownership has increased in a number of higher productivity sectors, such as ICT (51%), mining (18%) and professional and technical services (17%).

Difficulties in accessing finance and attracting investment may hold back productivity growth, innovation, and ultimately the competitiveness of SMEs. Despite concerted efforts to increase investment, levels of both domestic and foreign fixed capital formation remain low. The consequences for underinvestment in Kazakhstan are significant, particularly in the context of the digital and decarbonisation transitions, which require significant levels of capital-intensive modernisation. Within Kazakhstan, the major footprint of SOEs in the national banking sector, onerous collateral requirements and high market lending rates make access to finance one of the key challenges for the local private-sector. In 2020, the most recent year for which data are available, domestic credit to the private-sector equalled 25.6% GDP, and significantly below the OECD average of 160.7% (World Bank, 2023[2]). The shallowness of domestic credit is compounded by an underdeveloped domestic capital market, with the USD 45.3 billion market capitalisation of the Kazakhstan Stock Exchange (KASE) large for Central Asia but is dwarfed by more established exchanges elsewhere (KASE, 2023[22]). One result of access to finance challenges is that firms are heavily reliant on internal funds for financing needs, which may limit the scope of investment – and incentives for investing – at the firm level (Figure 2.9).

One of the consequences of difficult access to finance is the limited level of investment in ICTs and intangible capital at the firm-level, which may hold back productivity growth and competitiveness. Innovation, the major driver of competitiveness, requires both access to technologies and the infrastructure necessary to use them, and the intangible capital (skills, managerial ability, etc.) required to identify opportunities for innovation and to harness those opportunities. The level of investment in ICT is extremely low as a share of total investment and is significantly below the OECD average (1.98% GFCF vs. 11.4% OECD average) (National Statistical Office of Kazakhstan, 2023[23]). This may in part reflect the industrial structure of Kazakhstan, with key industries such as mining being extremely capital-intensive. It also highlights the broader difficulty of ensuring that the banking sector can channel capital resources to productivity-enhancing investments that benefit the wider economy, something that is made difficult by the onerous cost of borrowing for SMEs. Another channel through which access to finance difficulties affect the competitiveness of domestic firms is in innovation capacities. For example, in 2018, the last year for which data are available, gross domestic expenditure on R&D in Kazakhstan amounted to 0.12% GDP; the equivalent figures for the EU and the OECD were 2.1% and 2.4% respectively (OECD, 2023[24]). Relative to GDP, Kazakhstan is now spending half of what it spent on R&D in 2002, which will undoubtedly have an impact on the innovation, productivity and competitiveness of the local private-sector.

Despite a relatively open regulatory environment for investment, levels of FDI remain low. As a source of financing, FDI remains relatively small in Kazakhstan (Figure 2.9 a), and in 2020, FDI inflows were equal to 2% of GDP, with levels having fallen continuously relative to GDP since the Global Financial Crisis in 2008-09 (Figure 2.9 b). Mining and quarrying accounted for the largest share of FDI in 2020, with manufacturing and wholesale trade the industries that were the other two largest recipients (Fig. 2.9c). The largest investors in 2022 were the Netherlands (29.75%), the USA (18.23%), Switzerland (9.86%) and Belgium (5.57%); China accounted for 5.11% of the total. FDI tends to be concentrated in a handful of regions, notably Atyrau Region (29.4% in 2022), Almaty (27%, Astana (8%) and the East-Kazakhstan Region (7.9%), with the regional concentration of FDI relatively unchanged in recent years (National Statistical Office of Kazakhstan, 2023[23]).

Figure 2.9. Foreign direct investment in Kazakhstan

FDI plays a relatively small role in GFCF in Kazakhstan, and is concentrated in a handful of industries

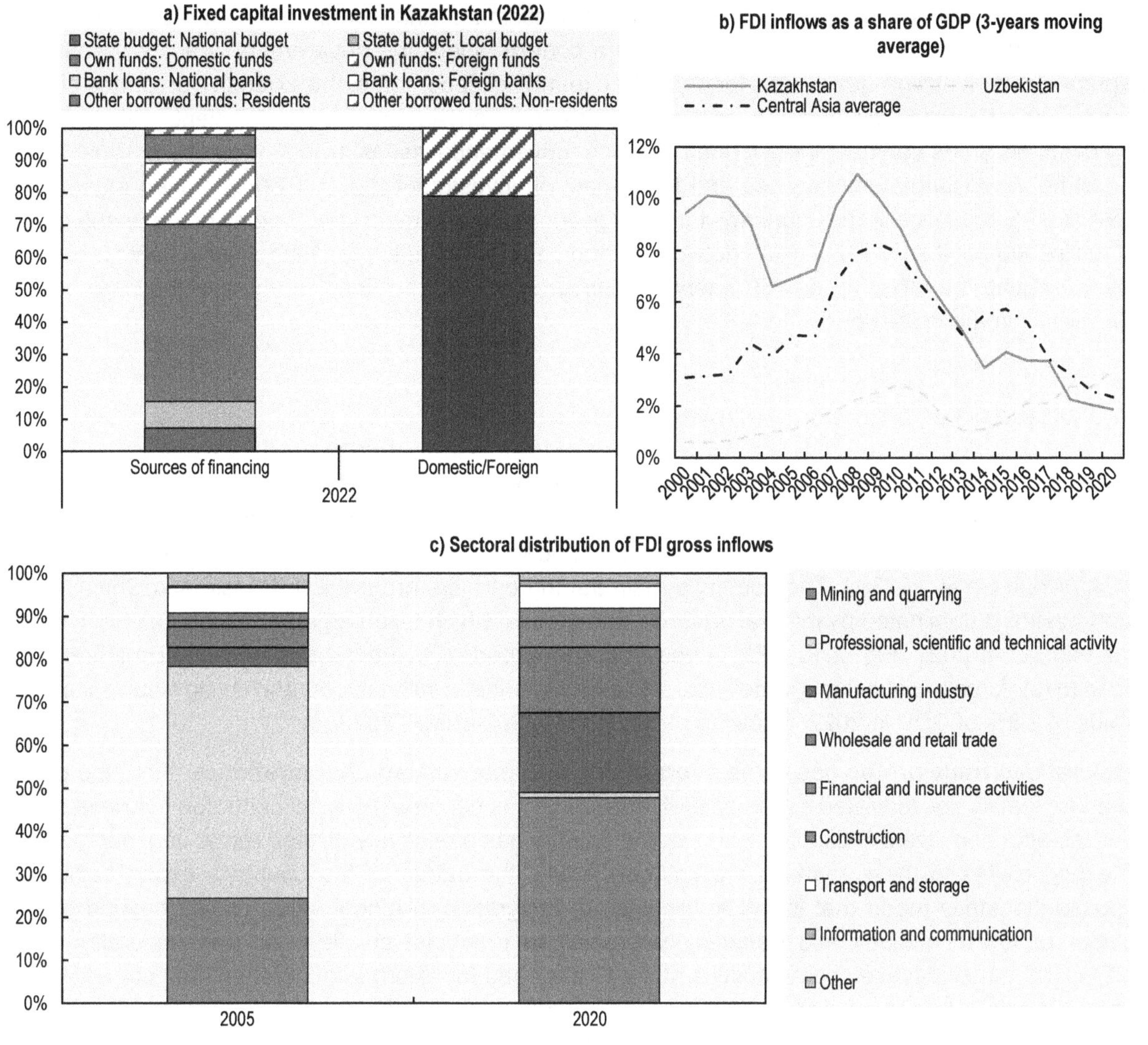

Source: OECD calculations based on data from (UNCTAD, 2023[25])

It is notable that the government has a wide-ranging policy programme to support privatisation, better corporate governance of SOEs, and to rationalise the role of the state in the economy more generally. Kazakhstan is therefore acutely aware of the importance of addressing these issues if the country is to transition to a more sustainable and inclusive model of growth. For example, in its *Comprehensive Privatisation Plan 2021-2025*, the government has listed 675 public and quasi-public bodies that will be privatised, liquidated or corporatised ahead of privatisation. The government also continues to work with the OECD on these issues, notably through projects on corporate governance of SOEs (OECD, 2021[26]).

The large direct role of the state in the economy may be another challenge for private-sector development. In the OECD Product Market Regulation indicators, Kazakhstan was ranked the fifth most restrictive economy in the countries covered by the index, the economy the third highest level of distortion due to state involvement, and the most restrictive economy in terms of public ownership (OECD, 2018[27]). Whilst the country scores well in areas such as the administrative barriers on start-ups, the playing field nevertheless appears to be highly uneven due to the widespread presence of the state in the economy, from the banking sector to key network sectors and major heavy industries, and the governance of SOEs.

The interaction between the role of the state in the economy and structural transformation towards a market economy is complex and multifaceted (Hausmann and Rodrik, 2003[28]) (Amsden, 2001[29]) (Ha-Joon (Ed.) and Rowthorn (Ed.), 1995[30]). In a context where the government is actively seeking to foster the creation of high-quality jobs for a rapidly expanding labour force, the extensive presence of SOEs creates myriad challenges that will continue to frustrate private-sector development: soft budgetary constraints on SOEs can contribute to inefficiencies, governance issues around incumbents, subsidies to support below cost-recovery services and the impact on investment (IMF, 2021[31]). Taken together, the extent of SOE presence in the economy, the poor governance and oversight of many of these enterprises, and the location of these SOEs in key network sectors, all contribute to make the playing field for business uneven, limiting the effectiveness of otherwise encouraging reform efforts to improve the business and investment climate in the country.

2.5. Trade and economic internationalisation

Kazakhstan became a member of the World Trade Organisation in 2015, and external trade is a major driver of growth and domestic output. In 2021, trade was equivalent to 58% of Kazakhstan's GDP while the export of goods and services amounted to 33.6% of GDP, against an OECD average of 28.2% (World Bank, 2023[2]). The country's main trading partners are the EU, Russia and China, and its export basket is dominated by mineral products and metals, which taken together accounted for over 80% of all exports in 2021 (Fig. 2.10). Revenues from the export of hydrocarbons and other minerals have helped to reinforce Kazakhstan's large fiscal and external buffers, with the country having a current account surplus of 2.8% of GDP in 2022, following a 4% deficit in 2021 (IMF, 2023[32]).

Kazakhstan's trade profile has three overarching and interrelated characteristics. First, the country has an extremely concentrated export basket, one which has become more concentrated overtime despite domestic efforts to diversify exports. Second, the country has a relatively diverse range of export partners, but export routes to these markets are limited. Finally, the nature of the country's export basket and domestic industries mean that it has a low level of integration in global value chains beyond being a provider of low-technology and generally unprocessed products, chiefly fuels and minerals (OECD, 2021[33]). All three of these characteristics attest to the need for reforms to increase the competitiveness of non-extractive industries and to raise the value-added of extractive industries by moving to more sophisticated activities that create higher productivity employment within those industries, and to improve the trade connectivity of the country to allow non-extractive sectors to be more competitive on global markets.

Minerals and metal products accounted for over 80% of all exports in 2022, and the concentration of Kazakhstan's export basket has grown over the past two decades (Figure 2.10). Kazakhstan made significant efforts to diversify range of products that it exports, but the diversification of products has made little impact to the overall concentration of exports in terms of value. Higher value-added capital goods such as machinery account for a very small share of the country's exports (around 1%) but are the single largest single category of imports (27.4%). In other words, the industrialisation and modernisation of Kazakhstan's is funded to a large extent by resource revenues.

Figure 2.10. Structure of trade: export basket and partners (2010 and 2019)

Kazakhstan's export basked has become more concentrated since 2000 despite the country exporting a broader range of products, while the share of the EU and China as export markets has grown significantly over the same period.

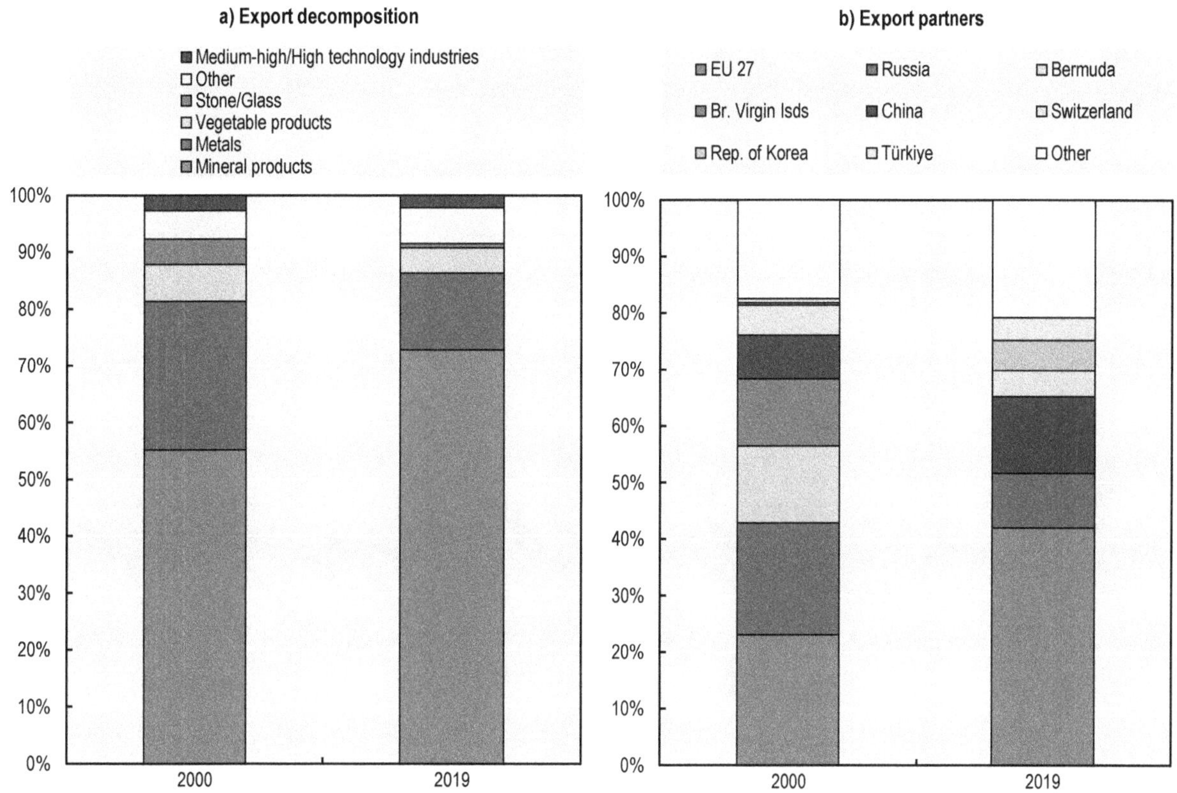

Source: OECD calculations based on data from (UN Comtrade, 2023[34])

In 2019, the EU was the largest market for Kazakhstan's exports, followed by China and Russia. The EU accounted for 42% of Kazakhstan's exports in 2019, while China accounted for 13.6% in the same year. While the EU market has grown significantly for Kazakhstan since 2000, **Kazakhstan has in recent years become increasingly oriented towards China and other Asian markets**. For example, Kazakhstan's exports to China grew 71.3% in 2015-2020, or by USD 3.9 billion in nominal terms; exports to India grew 682% over the same period, with this almost entirely attributable to oil exports. Exports to the EU have in fact fallen over the same period, particularly to the country's three largest EU partners, Italy (17.4%), the Netherlands (-36.7%) and France (-34%) (Observatory of Economic Complexity, 2023[16]).

Given the connectivity penalty Kazakhstan suffers, it is unsurprising that its largest trading partners for lower value-to-weight goods are geographically proximate, particularly the Central Asian economies. In recent years Kazakhstan has been actively exploring ways to diversify its trade routes, one example of this being the development of the Middle Corridor, with the importance of diversifying international trade routes increasing due to the significant volume of Kazakhstan's trade that transits Russia and the risk of secondary sanctions there (Kenderdine and Bucsky, 2021[35]).

Kazakhstan's inclusion in the OECD Trade in Value Added (TiVA) indicators allows for a more detailed look at the interaction between foreign demand and domestic output in Kazakhstan, as well as a more in depth look at the country's integration into global value chains (GVCs) than is possible for other Eurasia economies. In 2018, the most recent year for which TiVA data are available,

36.3% of Kazakhstan's domestic value added was driven by foreign final demand, though there was significant variation at the industrial level (OECD, 2021[33]). For example, the domestic value added in mining and quarrying is almost entirely driven by foreign demand (94.5%), which although logical given the size of that industry's output relative to domestic needs, is nevertheless indicative of the precarious relationship between output in the country's most productive sectors and external demand (Ibid.).

Figure 2.11. Domestic value added in foreign final demand (2018)

The value added of many key industries is driven by foreign demand

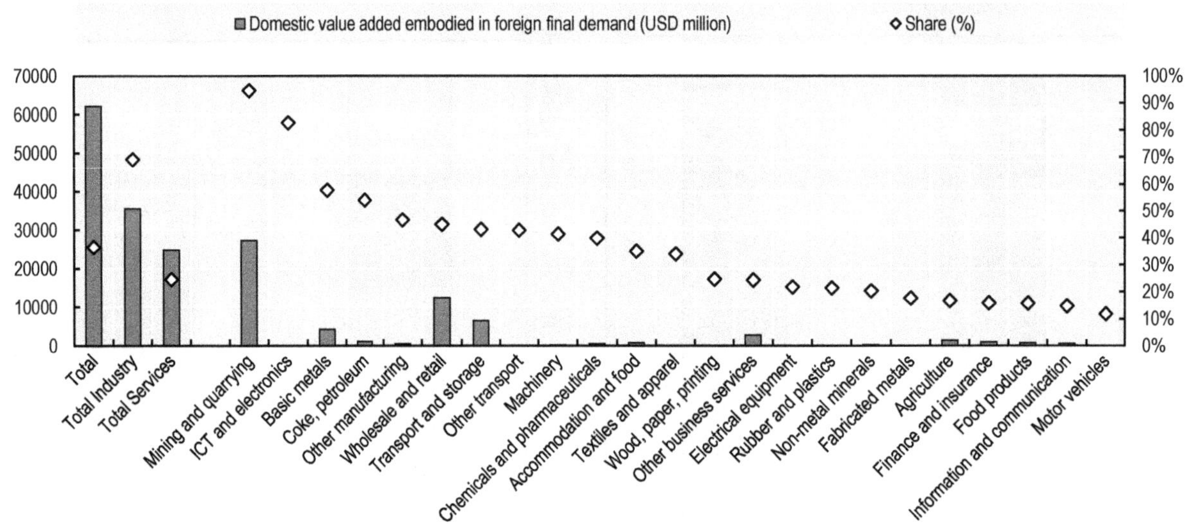

Source: OECD TiVA database Source: (OECD, 2021[33])

Given the low level of more sophisticated exports, the role of imports for exports – beyond the capital goods necessary for the extractive sector – is limited. There are a number of sectors where the foreign value added (FVA) content of exports – i.e., the extent to which a good exported by Kazakhstan has benefited from externally sourced inputs – but these are limited, and their overall contribution to gross exports – for example, ICT and electronics, rubber and plastics, or textiles – is low (Figure 2.11). This has a number of implications for Kazakhstan's trade, notably that it means that the value added of exports is generally created within Kazakhstan, rather than from reprocessed intermediate goods sources externally. The broader conclusion, however, is that the data highlight the very limited degree of integration of Kazakhstan in GVCs – the country has a small number of industries that are embedded in GVCs, particularly at more sophisticated stages of these GVCs, and its contribution to the value added of its export markets is primarily through fuel and other basic goods.

References

Amsden, A. (2001), *the rise of "the rest": Challenges to the west from late-industrializing economies*, Oxford University Press, https://doi.org/10.1093/0195139690.001.0001. [29]

Corden, M. and P. Neary (1982), *Booming Sector and De-Industrialisation in a Small Open Economy*, The Economic Journal, No. No. 368, pp. 825-848, https://doi.org/10.2307/2232670. [19]

EBRD (2022), *Kazakhstan Country Strategy 2022-2027*, EBRD. [6]

EBRD (2017), *Kazakhstan diagnostic paper: Assessing progress and challenges in developing a sustainable market economy*, EBRD, https://www.ebrd.com/publications/country-diagnostics. [5]

Frankel, J. and D. Romer (1999), *Does Trade Cause Growth?*, American Economic Review, No. 89(3):379-399, https://doi.org/10.1257/aer.89.3.379. [18]

Ha-Joon (Ed.), C. and R. Rowthorn (Ed.) (1995), *The Role of the State in Economic Change*, Oxford University Press, https://academic.oup.com/book/5167. [30]

Hausmann, R. and D. Rodrik (2003), *Economic Development as Self-Discovery*, Journal of Development Economics, No. 72(2), 602-633, https://growthlab.cid.harvard.edu/files/growthlab/files/2002_econ_development_self_discovery_hausmann_rodrik.pdf. [28]

IEA (2022), *Uzbekistan 2022: Energy Policy Review*, International Energy Agency, Paris, https://iea.blob.core.windows.net/assets/0d00581c-dc3c-466f-b0c8-97d25112a6e0/Uzbekistan2022.pdf. [11]

IEA (2022), *World Energy Outlook*, IEA, Paris, https://iea.blob.core.windows.net/assets/830fe099-5530-48f2-a7c1-11f35d510983/WorldEnergyOutlook2022.pdf. [10]

ILO (2023), *ILOSTAT*, ILO, Geneva, https://ilostat.ilo.org/. [9]

IMF (2023), *World Economic Outlook Database*, IMF, DC, https://www.imf.org/en/Publications/WEO/weo-database/2023/April. [32]

IMF (2022), *Republic of Kazakhstan: 2022 Article IV Consultation*, IMF, DC. [4]

IMF (2021), *State-Owned Enteprises in Middle East, North Africa, and Central Asia: Size, Costs, and Challenges*, IMF, DC, https://doi.org/10.5089/9781513594088.087. [31]

ITF (2019), *Enhancing Connectivity and Freight in Central Asia*, OECD Publishing, Paris, https://www.itf-oecd.org/sites/default/files/docs/connectivity-freight-central-asia_2.pdf. [21]

KASE (2023), *Kazakhstan Stock Exchange: Overview of KASE equity market in February 2023*, KASE, Astana, https://kase.kz/en/. [22]

Kenderdine, T. and P. Bucsky (2021), *Middle Corridor - Poliy Development and Trade Potential of the Trans-Caspian Transport Route*, ADBI Workign Paper Series, No. 1268, ADBI, https://www.adb.org/sites/default/files/publication/705226/adbi-wp1268.pdf. [35]

MacroTrends (2023), *Crude Oil Prices - 70 Year Historical Chart*, MacroTrends, https://www.macrotrends.net/1369/crude-oil-price-history-chart. [7]

National Statistical Office of Kazakhstan (2023), *Об инвестициях в основной капитал в Республике Казахстан (январь-февраль 2023г.)*, National Statistical Office of Kazakhstan, Astana, https://new.stat.gov.kz/ru/industries/business-statistics/stat-invest/publications/5194/. [23]

National Statistics Office of Kazakhstan (2023), *Enterprise Statistics*, National Statistics Office of Kazakhstan, Astana, https://new.stat.gov.kz/ru/industries/business-statistics/stat-org/. [20]

National Statistics Office of Kazakhstan (2023), *Main Indicators*, National Statistics Office of Kazakhstan, https://stat.gov.kz/official/industry/11/statistic/7. [8]

Observatory of Economic Complexity (2023), *Kazakhstan*, OEC, MIT, https://oec.world/en/profile/country/kaz#:~:text=Economic%20Complexity,-%23permalink%20to%20section&text=Kazakhstan%20has%20a%20high%20level,expected%20exports%20in%20each%20product. [16]

OECD (2023), *Air pollution exposure* (indicator), https://doi.org/10.1787/8d9dcc33-en (accessed on 20 April 2023). [14]

OECD (2023), *GERD as a percentage of GDP*, https://www.oecd.org/sti/scoreboard.htm. [24]

OECD (2023), *Green Growth Indicators*, OECD Publishing, Paris, https://stats.oecd.org/Index.aspx?DataSetCode=GREEN_GROWTH. [12]

OECD (2022), *Green Economy Transition in Eastern Europe, the Caucasus and Central Asia: Progress and Ways Forward*, OECD Green Growth Studies, OECD Publishing, Paris, https://www.oecd-ilibrary.org/docserver/c410b82a-en.pdf?expires=1677162424&id=id&accname=ocid84004878&checksum=F2BCEEF95E86BA77A3ACBB7C97571F14. [13]

OECD (2021), *Improving the Legal Environment for Business and Investment in Central Asia*, OECD Publishing, Paris, https://www.oecd.org/eurasia/Improving-LEB-CA-ENG%2020%20April.pdf. [1]

OECD (2021), *Ownership and Governance of State-Owned Enterprises: A Compendium of National Practices 2021*, OECD Publishing, Paris, https://www.oecd.org/corporate/Ownership-and-Governance-of-State-Owned-Enterprises-A-Compendium-of-National-Practices-2021.pdf. [26]

OECD (2021), *Trade in Value Added (TiVA) 2021 ed: Principal Indicators*, OECD Publishing, Paris, https://stats.oecd.org/Index.aspx?DataSetCode=TIVA_2021_C1. [33]

OECD (2020), *OECD Tax Policy Reviews: Kazakhstan 2020*, OECD Publishing, Paris, https://www.oecd-ilibrary.org/docserver/872d016c-en.pdf?expires=1679396564&id=id&accname=ocid84004878&checksum=5537B095685026BCB89BE0C725439AC0. [17]

OECD (2018), *The Regulation of Goods and Services Markets in Kazakhstan: An International Comparison in 2018*, OECD Publishing, Paris, https://www.oecd.org/economy/reform/indicators-of-product-market-regulation/. [27]

UN (2023), *Value added by industries at current prices (ISIC REV. 4)*, United Nations, New York, http://data.un.org/Data.aspx?d=SNA&f=group_code%3A204. [15]

UN Comtrade (2023), *UN Comtrade Database*, UN Comtrade, Geneva, https://comtrade.un.org/. [34]

UNCTAD (2023), *Foreign direct investment: Inward and outward flows and stock, annual*, UNCTAD, Geneva, https://unctadstat.unctad.org/wds/TableViewer/tableView.aspx?ReportId=96740. [25]

UNCTAD (2023), *UNCTATStat*, UNCTAD, Geneva, https://unctadstat.unctad.org/EN/. [3]

World Bank (2023), *World Bank Development Indicators*, World Bank, DC, https://databank.worldbank.org/source/world-development-indicators. [2]

Notes

[1] The regional average includes Kazakhstan, Kyrgyzstan, Tajikistan and Uzbekistan, but excludes Turkmenistan.

3 Survey methodology and findings overview

The purpose of the survey on Kazakhstan's business climate, conducted by the OECD in 2022, was to collect new firm-level insights into the ongoing reform process to support the private sector in the country. The survey provides additional insights for the OECD, the EU and the Government to consider when reflecting on the effectiveness and direction of the reform process. This chapter introduces the survey, its methodology, and a number of high-level observations that emerged from the process.

3.1. Introduction

This section introduces the business climate assessment survey (the "survey") for Kazakhstan and outlines some general observations that emerge from the results. Section 3.2 outlines the methodology of the survey and details how it was administered, while section 3.3. details the business demography of the sample firms. Section 3.4 then provides additional information on firms' perceptions of current economic trends, the impact of COVID-19 and Russia's war in Ukraine on the business climate in Kazakhstan, and the perceived strengths and limitations of policy interventions to support them during these periods of disruption.

3.2. Survey methodology and administration

The survey was small but focused, addressing 27 firms active in Kazakhstan, with the majority being wholly or partly owned by entities based in the EU. It presented an opportunity to gather bottom-up, firm-level perceptions on issues relating to the business climate and private-sector development in Kazakhstan. In addition to the surveyed firms, the survey was also completed by four trade or business organisations from OECD countries active in Kazakhstan.

The survey was developed by the OECD and administered via an online platform to foreign businesses and their representatives in Chambers of Commerce (CCs) or Embassies. The consultation of primarily European businesses was designed to identify issues of particular importance to international firms, the attraction of which remains a priority for the government. Throughout this report, analysis of survey responses, unless otherwise indicated, is based on the responses of both the 27 individual firms and the four organisational respondents.

3.3. Characteristics of surveyed firms

The characteristics of the 27 firms that took part in the survey were highly (Figure 3.1). Most respondent firms have been established in Kazakhstan for a relatively long time, perhaps indicative of a certain confidence in the country's business climate. Half of respondents had been active for 20 years or more; 30% of respondents had been active for up to 10 years, meaning that a significant number of respondents were relatively new to the country; 22% of respondents had been active for 11-19 years.

The ownership and legal structure of the respondents was also varied. The ownership of almost two thirds of the surveyed firms (63%) was 100% based in the EU. The ownership of the remaining firms was either 50% American, 50% British, or from a different jurisdiction or combinations thereof (22%). The Netherlands accounted for the single largest share of respondents (10/37%), followed by Germany (4/15%). A similarly large plurality of firms had LLC status (63%), with the remaining firms having a range of different legal statuses, including representative offices (16%) or JSCs (7%).

The respondents represented a diverse range of sectors, but two of them were slightly more represented: machinery and equipment (8/30%) and agriculture (5/19%). Other sectors, such as mining, oil and gas, ICT, wholesale and retail, were almost evenly represented but with lower shares.

Figure 3.1. Demographics of respondent firms

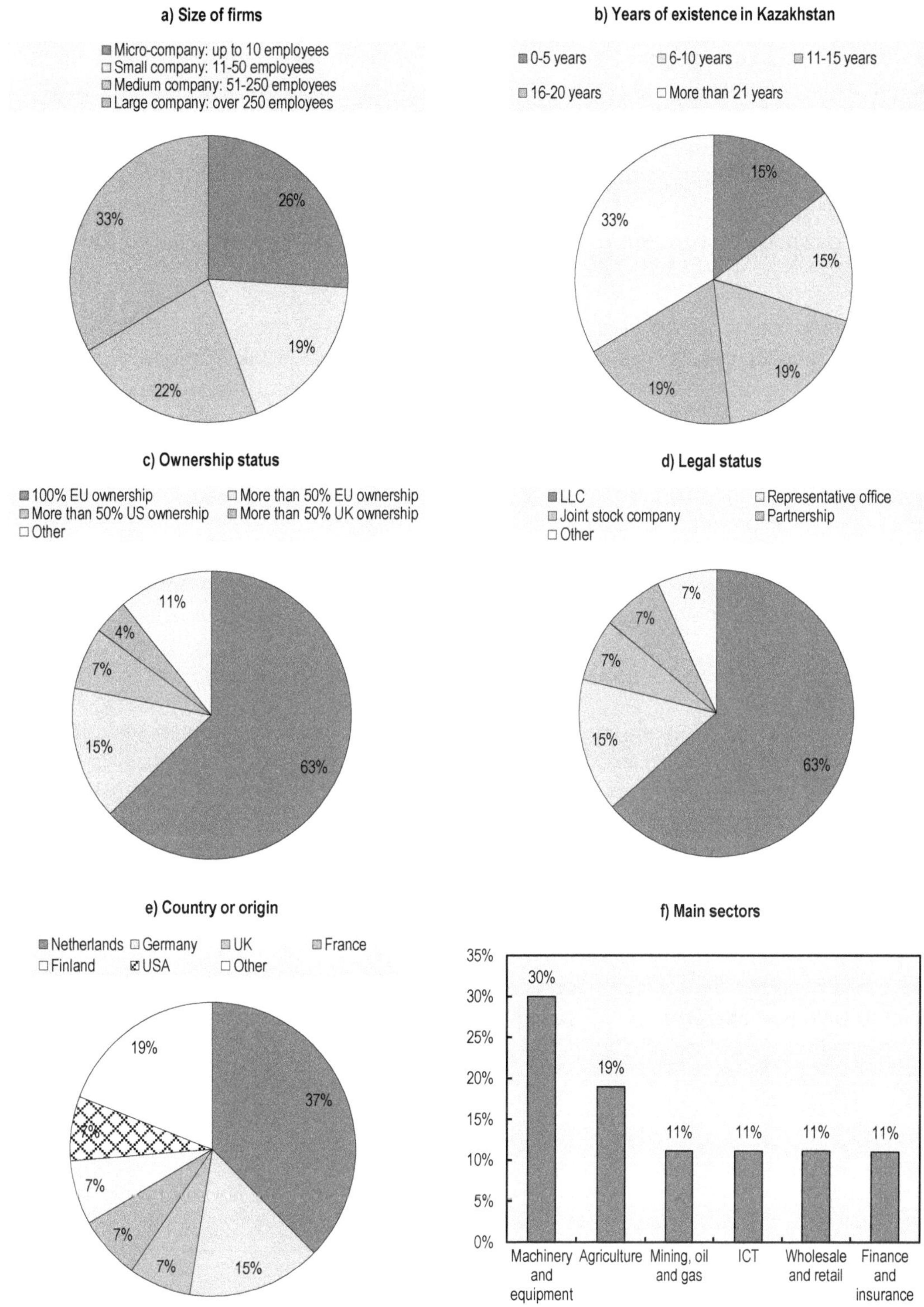

Note: As a percent of the total number of firms. Main sectors do not add up to 100% since it was possible for the respondents to answer to multiple choices.
Source: EU-OECD Business Climate Assessment Survey in Kazakhstan (2022)

3.4. High level observations on economic performance in Kazakhstan and recent policy support

This section presents key insights from five sections of the survey: firms perceptions of the overall economic situation in Kazakhstan, of government support during the COVID-19 pandemic, of the impact of Russia's war on Ukraine on the European business community in the country, of government measures to mitigate pressures on the business community arising due to war-related disruptions, and of the ongoing reform process.

3.4.1. On the economic situation in the context of COVID-19 and Russia's war of aggression

A majority of respondents (58%) rated the health of the national economy as satisfactory. However, none of the firms reported that it was strong, while 42% said that it was weak. There was greater positivity from respondents when asked to assess the performance of the sector in which they were active or the performance of their own firm (16% weak for both items).

Firms remained positive about their businesses in the post-COVID context. Almost the half of respondents (48%) reported that they expected an increase in profits, with a further 39% reporting that they expected their performance to remain stable. Only 10% anticipated a decrease in profits for 2022. Only 3% (including trade associations and embassies representing several firms) anticipated that trade turnover (domestic and international) would decrease, whereas 23% of respondents expected international trade turnover to increase, and 42% expected domestic (wholesale and retail) trade turnover to increase.

3.4.2. Support to the business sector during the COVID-19 pandemic

The outbreak of COVID-19 created significant challenges for the business community in Kazakhstan, as it did throughout Central Asia and the OECD area. These challenges also created new expectations of government, which was called on to ensure the survival of viable businesses and prevent their unnecessary exit from the market. The design and implementation of policy interventions to this end required a high degree of agility from policymakers, who were required to make quick, effective decisions in a context of heightened uncertainty and fiscal constraints.

The Kazakh authorities intervened in different ways to protect the economy during the pandemic, including the issuance of state-guaranteed loans, tax deferrals, and direct compensation of certain business costs for firms. The type of support of offered by the government to the business community was similar to what was offered in OECD countries, albeit on a different scale. These interventions were widely discussed in a number of OECD reports throughout 2020-21, and the survey provided an opportunity to gauge how European firms assessed the effectiveness of government policies to stabilise and support the private sector throughout this period of significant disruption (OECD, 2020[1]) (OECD, 2021[2]).

Figure 3.2. Government's measures effectiveness against the COVID-19 pandemic according to the respondents

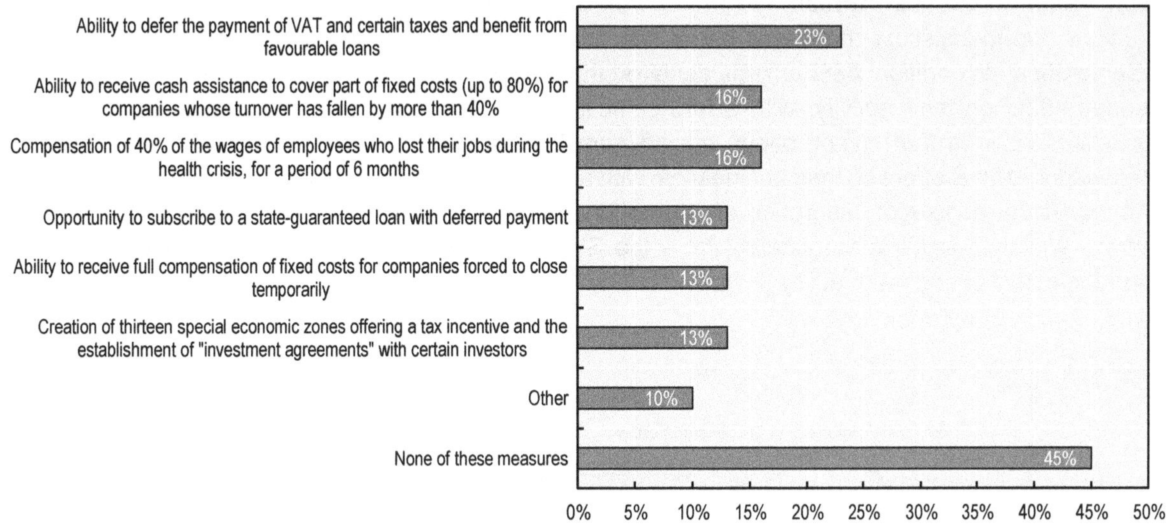

Note: As a percent of the total number of respondents.
Source: EU-OECD Business Climate Assessment Survey on Kazakhstan (2022)

Among the respondents, the single most popular measure taken by the government was the deferral of VAT and other tax payments (23% of firms approved). Direct wage subsidies were considered useful by 16% respondents, and the same figure considered useful the ability to receive cash payments to cover immediate fixed costs. Perhaps most striking, however, is that 45% of the surveyed firms considered none of the measures taken by the government that were mentioned in the survey to be useful, which suggests either that policy intervention was directed to areas where business needs were less pressing, or that the measures taken did not go far enough, or that foreign firms were not the targets.

3.4.3. The impact of Russia's war on European firms in Kazakhstan

Russia's war in Ukraine delivered another significant shock to the business community in Kazakhstan, both in terms of its domestic and international firms, which was transmitted via the same channels as in many OECD countries: supply chain disruptions, rising prices for primary and intermediate goods, inflation, and a tightening in the global financial system that affected international and local borrowing costs. In addition, these impact channels were mapped onto local circumstances that were peculiar to the region: the particularly large importance of Russia as a trading partner and as a route for exports for Central Asian economies, the interconnectedness of Central Asian banking systems with Russia, the immediate impact of both low- and high-skilled immigration from Russia, the potential for a stagnant Russian economy to affect remittance levels, and the impact of turmoil in the Russian economy on local exchange rates. In Kazakhstan, where the vast majority of its hydrocarbon exports transit Russia, disruptions to trade routes through Russia were particularly challenging, and the possibility of additional disruptions remains a significant source of uncertainty as the war continues.

The survey indicates that one of the main issues that businesses had to face early on was related to the volatility of the Tenge and the instability of the foreign exchange market. Some 58% of respondents assessed its impact as serious for their operations, with a further 29% claiming that it had some effect on their operations. Firm concerns over currency volatility reflect a longer-standing challenge for the business climate in Kazakhstan, where macroeconomic uncertainty can erode business confidence and make it more difficult for firms to commit to investing in the country.

Supply-chain issues also threatened firms' operations. Some 52% of respondents claimed that the disruptions due to logistical challenges had a serious effect on their operations, and 45% claimed that it has some effect. In addition, 48% of firms declared that disruptions in supply chains due to shortages had a serious effect on their activity, with a further 35% claiming that it had some effect. Finally, 48% of respondents claimed that complications arising from Russia's disconnection from the SWIFT payment system had a serious effect on their businesses, with another 23% claiming it had some effect. This testifies to the significant degree of integration of international firms in Central Asia with the Russian economy. However, whilst Russia's disconnection from the SWIFT system had a serious impact on the half of respondents, it also had no effect on 26%.

Figure 3.3. Firms' reactions to Russia's war and assessment of governmental measures

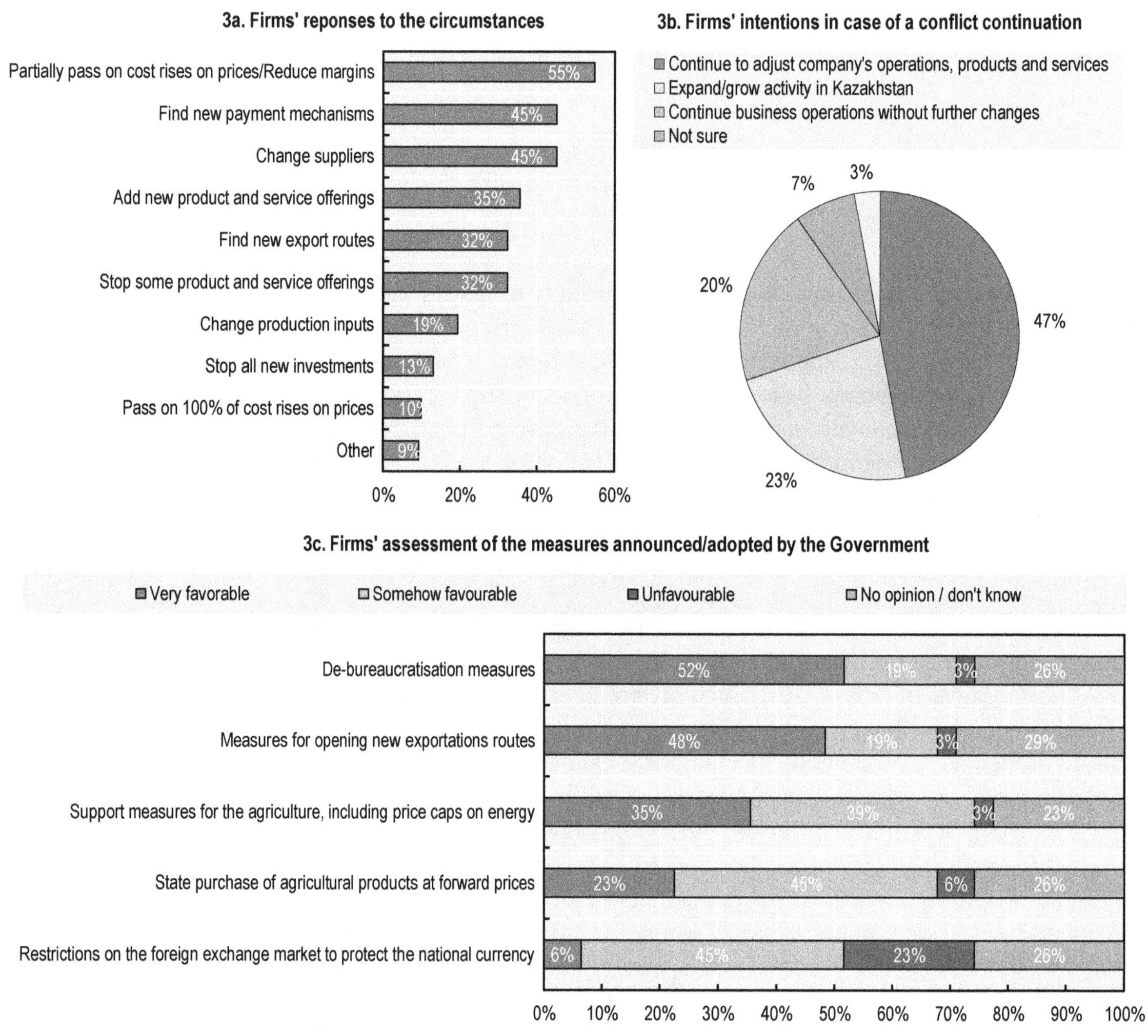

Source: EU-OECD Business Climate Assessment Survey in Kazakhstan (2022)

Input costs for raw materials such as energy as well as other intermediary inputs have risen. A large majority of respondents declared that they have been negatively impacted by rising commodity prices

(84%), energy prices (81%) as well as non-commodity prices (77%). In other words, only a minority of firms were unaffected by price increases (less than 16% for each category).

The survey respondents outlined a number of possible responses to the challenges posed by Russia's war in Ukraine for Kazakhstan's business community. A majority of respondents demonstrated agility in meeting these challenges, with 55% claiming that they would partially pass on cost rises and reduce margins, 45% responding that they would change suppliers, and 45% claiming that they would find new payment mechanisms. A third of firms indicated that the crisis would encourage them to innovate, with 35% responding that they planned to offer new products or services. At the same time, 32% of respondents would rather stop some product and service offerings, and 32% responded that they would find new export routes. Only a small number of respondents indicated their intention to change production inputs (19%), and fewer still to stop investment (13%) or pass on 100% of cost increases (10%).

Respondents appeared committed to the Kazakh market, regardless of whether the war were to continue or not. Only 3% reported that they would suspend operations in the country until the situation improved, while 47% reported that they would adjust their operations to developments as they unfolded and another 23% claimed that they would continue with their current course of action regardless of a prolongation of the war (Figure 3.3 b) An additional 20% of respondents claimed that they would expand their activities in the country should the war continue, though it is not clear whether this was because of the war, or whether pre-existing expansion plans had simply not been derailed.

3.4.4. Support to the business sector following Russia's invasion of Ukraine

Interpretation of firms' assessments of interventions from the Kazakh authorities to support the business sector must be qualified by the fact that, unlike the primarily retrospective assessment of the effectiveness of measures to support firms through the COVID-19 pandemic, the impact channels of Russia's war in Ukraine on firms in Ukraine are still being defined, and the full effects remain unclear. Addressing the challenges faced by firms in Kazakhstan that have arisen due to Russia's war will require the government to demonstrate the same agility and creativity as it did during the COVID-19 pandemic, but the policy areas requiring intervention will at times be very different (for example, measures to mitigate disruption in the banking sector, or labour market policies to integrate recent arrivals).

It is notable that approximately a quarter of respondents did not know or expressed no opinion on each of the measures listed in the survey. Otherwise, the strongest support was for de-bureaucratisation measures (52% very favourably and 19% somewhat favourably), as well as for measures to open new export routes (48% very favourably and 10% somewhat favourably). Two other measures were also supported by a majority of respondents, such as the support for agriculture, including price caps on energy (35% very favourably and 39% somewhat favourably), and the state purchase of agricultural products at forward prices (23% very favourably and 45% somewhat favourably). The last measure listed in the survey, concerning restrictions on the foreign exchange market to protect the national currency, was strongly approved by only 6% of the respondents but 45% were somehow favourable. The other half of respondents was either unfavourable (23%) or did not know/had no opinion (26%).

Only 43% of respondents considered that the measures implemented by the government to alleviate pressures on the business sector arising from the war were satisfying. For the remaining 57%, other measures should be considered, related to the tax system, banking and financial system and trade policies. Most of the measures proposed by the respondents are not always an answer to the war in Ukraine but rather structural, reflecting broader concerns about the business climate and framework conditions for firms. If the wish for a better regulation of the currency or the development of new transport routes (to the European Union, Middle East or China) might be seen as an answer to the war in Ukraine, the development of trade through new export routes is not only confined to such periods but can also help to diversify and enhance Kazakhstan's economy in the longer term. Moreover, issues related to tax pressure and the stability of the tax system, or the desire to have easier access to finance, are measures that would be related to long-standing issues in the business climate of the country. Indeed, these issues have been much discussed in OECD work on the business climate in Kazakhstan and Central Asia more broadly (OECD, 2021[3]).

Calls from certain respondents to increase access to non-Russian goods through new trade routes reflect the importance of the Russian market for Kazakh firms, both in terms of finished and intermediate goods. The inability of firms to use Russian suppliers, whether due to sanctions or other logistical difficulties, invariably has an effect on Kazakh firms, but it is not necessarily a weakness of the local business climate so long as firms do not face policy barriers to sourcing inputs from other markets. It does, however, reflect the importance of questions such as infrastructure and trade facilitation as enablers of the local private sector. At the same time, respondents' calls for the elimination of grey imports does suggest inconsistent implementation of customs procedures which could unfairly affect European firms in the country.

References

OECD (2021), *Beyond COVID-19: Prospects for Economic Recovery in Central Asia*, OECD Publishing, Paris, https://www.oecd.org/eurasia/Beyond_COVID%2019_Central%20Asia.pdf. [2]

OECD (2021), *Improving the Legal Environment for Business and Investment in Central Asia*, OECD Publishing, Paris, https://www.oecd.org/eurasia/Improving-LEB-CA-ENG%2020%20April.pdf. [3]

OECD (2020), *COVID-19 Crisis Response in Central Asia*, OECD Publishing, Paris, https://read.oecd-ilibrary.org/view/?ref=129_129634-ujyjsqu30i&title=COVID-19-crisis-response-in-central-asia. [1]

4 Addressing infrastructure and skills gaps for private sector digitalisation

Government efforts to improve digital infrastructure and the digitalisation of public service delivery were received positively by survey respondents. The government has made significant progress in these areas in recent years, and digitalisation remains a cornerstone of its ambitions to develop economic competitiveness, raise productivity and foster innovation. Yet, despite an improved supply of digital services and infrastructure, the diffusion of digital tools and processes at the firm level remains limited. This chapter highlights achievements that the government has made in facilitating the digital transition, notably in its success with e-government and digital public service delivery, before highlighting a number of challenges relating to infrastructure and skills for the digital transformation.

4.1. Overview and survey insights

The digital transformation can have a profound impact on private sector development (OECD, 2021[1]). Digitalisation can offer new opportunities for firm organisation and production, as well as how crucial government services are administered, while the ever-increasing value of data as an economic input is pushing the frontiers of innovation in both the public and private sectors. At the same time, as the contribution of digital technologies and services continues to increase its share of value added in both manufacturing and services, who has the skills and capacities to take advantage of digitalisation, as well as where those skills and capacities are located, has significant implications for competitiveness, inclusion, and inequality.

Many survey respondents underscored their enthusiasm for digital opportunities in Kazakhstan but also expressed their frustration at how underdeveloped framework conditions prevented them from making the most of these opportunities. This is an important and positive observation – the surveyed firms remain dedicated to the Kazakh market, but believe that they can achieve more if the government is more responsive to their infrastructure and connectivity needs. Some 80% of respondents considered digitalisation to present opportunities for their business activities in Kazakhstan (40% significant opportunities, 40% some opportunities).

While only 7% of respondents reported that their firms had become fully digitalised, an overwhelming majority of firms had nevertheless adopted digital processes within their firms. Over half (54%) of respondents reported that upwards of 75% of internal processes now had some kind of digital component, while another 39% reported that 50-75% of internal processes now had a digital component. These figures suggest a fair level of digital penetration in the European business community in Kazakhstan, though it would be necessary to compare with the domestic business community with a larger sample size to determine whether such levels were representative throughout the country.

A significant number of respondents demonstrated an advanced level of digital maturity. For example, some 89% of respondents reported that they used advanced tools such as customer relationship manager software (CRM) or some form of data analytics, which suggests a relatively high level of digital maturity of European firms operating in Kazakhstan. The rate of firms using cloud-based data solutions (67%) and digital communications (70%) further underscores the digitalisation of the surveyed firms.

The key barrier to further adoption and use of digital technologies by the surveyed firms appears to be infrastructure-related. A majority (61%) of respondents underscored the importance of improving internet speed and quality for digitalisation, 52% emphasised the need to improve the terms provided by Internet providers to customers, and almost half (48%) highlighted the need to improve data security. Other issues related to the need to develop online payment systems (32%), improve the digital skills and qualifications of the labour force (23%), and improve the quality of the regulatory framework for online commerce (29%).

Enabling the private sector – and society more broadly – to make the most of the opportunities of the digital transformation requires a range of different policy interventions. For one, firms can only digitise their activities – for example, through the adoption of IT solutions, be they simple or advanced, to improve productivity – if the basic digital and connectivity infrastructure is in place. This means having access to high-quality fixed and cellular internet, and access to ICT equipment and software, as well as the availability of more complex forms of digital infrastructure, such as cloud computing. It also means having access to the skills and knowledge necessary to apply digital technologies and to derive new insights and innovations from them. And, importantly, it means having access to the capital necessary to invest in the above, and a regulatory environment which fosters digitalisation rather than constraints it.

On the supply side, infrastructure challenges can be linked to competition issues in key network sectors of the economy necessary to develop a modern, digital and connected economy. On the demand side, long-standing access to finance challenges may make it difficult for firms to invest in digital technologies and intangible capital necessary to make the most of them. The government of Kazakhstan has stated its ambition to drive the digital transformation of the country's economy, with its strategic objectives codified in the National Development Strategy project, as well as digital-specific strategies such as the 2018-2022 Digital Kazakhstan programme (OECD, 2023[2]).

This chapter builds upon research that the OECD conducted in 2023 on the digital framework conditions for Kazakhstan's private sector (OECD, 2023[3]). Insights from the survey complement a number of findings that emerged in this work, such as the demand from the private sector for improvements to connectivity infrastructure, and the need for greater regulatory clarity if firms are to make the most of the opportunities presented by the digital transformation. The policy implications of these challenges relate to the more transversal issues of competition in the telecommunications sector, access to finance for digital and other intangible investments, and regulatory quality and simplification.

This chapter gives an overview of the latest developments in private sector digitalisation in Kazakhstan, noting the particular improvements in the areas of digital public service delivery. It then expands upon two areas identified in the survey as challenging for firm-level digitalisation. First, the framework conditions for private sector digitalisation. Second, the skills-related challenges for firm-level adoption of digital tools, building on recent OECD work in this area (OECD, 2023[4]).

4.2. Digitising the state: a key success of Kazakhstan's digital agenda

The digitalisation of Kazakhstan's economy has been a policy priority and a major part of the country's diversification agenda since 2013, when the government launched its first major digital strategy "Informational Kazakhstan 2020" (Government of Kazakhstan, 2017[5]). This first digital strategy focused on the development of ICT infrastructure and online public administration systems to facilitate business activity (egov.kz, 2021[6]) and has been successful in developing country-wide connectivity. In 2018, the government followed this initial strategy with the five-year "Digital Kazakhstan" initiative, aimed at increasing the private sector's use of digital tools to support economic growth through targeted programmes in the agricultural, energy, transport, and e-commerce sectors, and which ran until 2022 (OECD, 2023[2]) (Digital Kazakhstan, 2022[7]). The initiative also developed additional sub-programmes, targeting digital innovation (launch of the Astana Hub International Technology Park in 2018) and cybersecurity ("Cybershield Kazakhstan"). In early 2022, the government launched "Digital Era Lifestyle" (*DigitEL*), its third five-year digitalisation programme, with a focus on quality and safe internet, using ICT businesses as a growth lever, and further digitalising the services sector (Republic of Kazakhstan, 2022[8]). DigitEL targets include an ICT share of GDP of 5%, compared to 4% in 2020, and the strategy anticipates greater involvement of the private sector, as over 70% of the programme is to be funded through private investments.

One area where the government has had great success with its digitalisation agenda has been e-government and digital public service delivery. Quality digital government services are important for improving the efficiency of interaction with state bodies in any country, but this is particularly true in a country like Kazakhstan, where low population density and a high degree of administrative centralisation can significantly raise the costs and time involved in accessing public services. Until it elapsed in 2022, the country's e-government agenda was guided by the Digital Kazakhstan strategy, which set a goal of providing 100% of government services online. As suggested through survey responses on the quality of service provision such as licensing and permits for businesses, these reforms appear to be bearing fruit.

In 2022, Kazakhstan had risen to 28th in the UN E-Government Development index, ahead of a number of OECD countries (United Nations, 2022[9]). The country's strong performance reflects a number of important, and at times challenging, reforms. Kazakhstan recognised the need to centralise public service delivery on a unified platform, but also took the opportunity in doing so to create adjacent platforms and services, such as an interoperable API and permitting linkages between government data and private partners (for example, in the banking sector), to improve previously analogue services and ensure that the digitisation process was harnessed as a moment to modernise service delivery comprehensively.

Kazakhstan has increasingly been applying data analysis to improve the policy process, particularly for policies that aim to improve the quality and coverage of digital infrastructure networks. For instance, under the NDS, citizen-reporting platforms have been created as a monitoring tool for minimum internet speed requirements imposed on operators in remote rural and small urban areas (Government of Kazakhstan, 2017[5]). The online platform gathers complaints about internet quality and is linked to the Interdepartmental Commission on Radio Frequencies and local state telecom authorities. It verifies connection quality and fines telecom operators immediately should quality fall below the minimum threshold.[1] OECD interviews suggest that the system has enabled the improvement of internet connection quality, especially in Kazakhstan's areas. The MIID has also developed monthly public-private dialogue (PPD) with the Council of Operators since 2020, where the owners of main telecommunication infrastructure and towers and large business associations discuss infrastructure bottlenecks and challenges. However, neither regional governments nor small last-mile operators are part of such meetings, which limits their effectiveness in gathering the relevant actors – national and local operators, regional authorities, and the private sector – to address often highly localised issues.

In addition, one of the main objectives of DigitEL is the development of data-driven government by 2025. The "attentive and effective state" initiative aims at creating a unified data collection process to ground policy decisions, including the development of user feedback for public services, and more importantly the automatic collection and treatment of data relevant for policy-making. However, in its current state, the initiative only targets industrial data to be monitored by the public revenue committee (Government of Kazakhstan, 2021[10]). If effective, the initiative could be expanded in the coming years to new sectors, where it could thereby serve as an important tool for gathering data about the digital needs and use of businesses.

4.3. Infrastructure and investment gaps remain a challenge to private sector digitalisation

The rate and depth of digitalisation in Kazakhstan, as in any country, is shaped by a number of important infrastructure-related framework conditions and the diffusion of digital technologies. It is precisely the lack of development of these framework conditions that survey respondents identified as being the major barrier to digitalisation in the country.

Kazakhstan continues to have a highly regulated telecommunications sector, with significant competition-related issues that may affect investment and the quality of connectivity infrastructure, slowing the rate of digitalisation. The government has made efforts to liberalise the sector, notably following accession to the WTO in 2015, when it lifted a monopoly on the provision of 4G services in the telecoms sector (OECD, 2023[3]). Before this point, only Altel, a subsidiary of *Kazakhtelecom*, had the right to provide 4G services. Since early 2017, all three mobile telephone providers have been allowed to get licenses on existing and new 4G frequencies (Samruk Kazyna, 2016[11]). In March 2021, *Kazakhstan Transtelecom*, a fixed broadband network operator and former subsidiary of the state-owned rail firm, was privatised. This followed a gradual process initiated in 2014, when the company was first included in a list of strategic assets for privatisation, before 49% of its shares were sold in 2015, followed by a second sale (26% of shares) in 2018 (Government of Kazakhstan, 2014[12]; Kazinform, 2015[13]).

In 2023, recognising the important role of small operators in bridging the "last-mile" connectivity gap, the OECD recommended that the government initiate steps to demonopolise that segment of internet provision (OECD, 2023[3]). While this should enable small operators to enter the mobile market, it remains unclear whether it aims at fostering end-to-end infrastructure competition, or if it is to allow for infrastructure sharing. In the first case, different operators, both new and incumbents, would compete with their own networks, while in the latter, small operators would use the infrastructure of incumbents but provide services to market segments that remain outside the current network, i.e. mainly in rural and small urban areas.

In the framework of this reform, the government announced that *Kazakhtelecom* would sell one of its two mobile operators in 2022, which would result in essentially three independent operators in the mobile market by the end of that year (Government of Kazakhstan, 2022[14]). In addition, the government set up a special Commission on demonopolisation in early 2022, with the main goal of reviewing and proposing amendments to the current legislation applicable to the telecom sector. The Commission is composed of the Ministries of Infrastructure Development and Justice, relevant public institutions, such as the Competition Authority, and representatives of the private sector. However, results have not yet been communicated and it is unclear if the partial privatisation of *Kazakhtelecom*'s mobile operators will result from the Commission's activities.

Nevertheless, since the early 2000s, the government has had significant success in developing and modernising the country's connectivity infrastructure, leading to affordable and quality access to internet in most of Kazakhstan's urban centres. In terms of access, nearly universal mobile coverage has been in place since 2015 at least, with the population covered by 2G or higher networks reaching 98% in 2019, while access to broadband internet remains more modest (ITU, 2022[15]). Internet access has also become widely affordable across the country, with fixed and mobile subscription costs falling in recent years; they are now well below the UNESCO's affordability target of 2% of Gross National Income (GNI) per capita. Fixed subscription costs stood at 0.85% of GNI per capita in 2020 (Figure 4.1) compared to a 2.3% average for the Commonwealth of Independent States (CIS), while mobile subscriptions costs are among the lowest in the world at 0.33% of GNI per capita, compared to 1.0% in CIS countries and 2.6% globally (ITU, 2022[15]; ITU, 2021[16]; Cable, 2022[17]).

Figure 4.1. Cost of fixed broadband access as percentage of GNI (2021

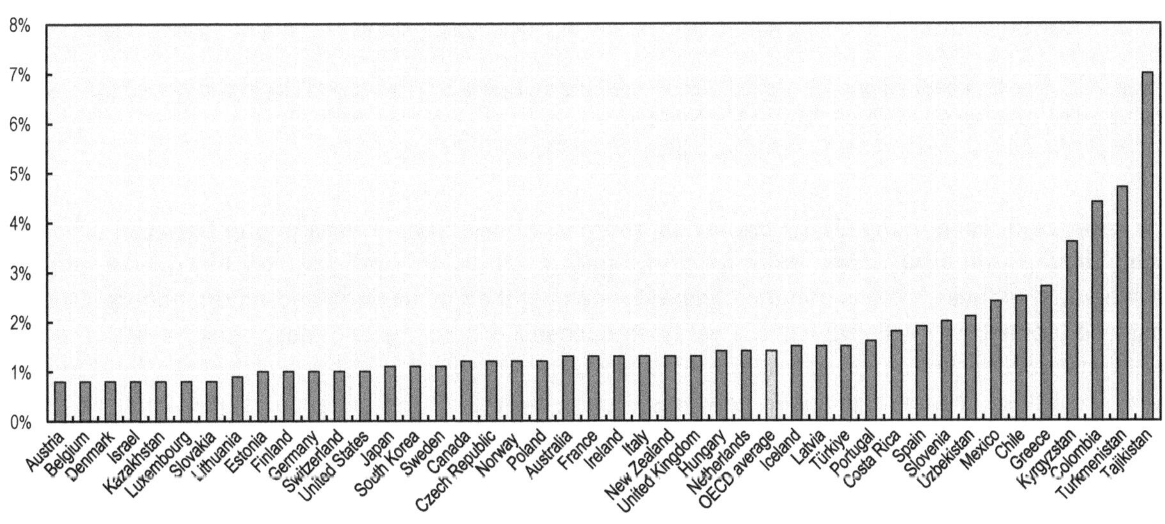

Source: (ITU, 2023[18])

Improvements have also been made in network quality. About three quarters of the population covered by 4G internet in 2021, while the download and upload speeds of broadband lines have doubled on average since 2017 (EIU, 2022[19]). Digital connectivity at large has also progressed in Kazakhstan, with a significant reduction in the rural-urban connectivity gap[2], with 89% of the rural and 91% of the urban population having access to broadband networks in 2019 (ITU, 2022[20]).

While fixed internet is a key driver for SME digitalisation, broadband uptake in Kazakhstan remains low compared to OECD countries. Broadband subscriptions per 100 households rose only slightly, from 13.1 in 2015 to 13.8 in 2021, compared to 33 on average in high-income countries (ITU, 2022[20]; OECD, n.d.[21]). Though there are no data available on small businesses specifically, only 7.8% of medium and large enterprises reported having access to fixed broadband internet in 2020 (Figure 4.2), while 48% of small business indicated having a website in the latest World Bank Enterprise survey, compared to almost 90% for large businesses (World Bank, 2021[22]). Access to fixed broadband internet varies widely among regions, ranging from 4.3% in Aktobe Region to 15.2% in neighbouring Atyrau. In 2019, the number was even lower (5.9%), with the recent increase being presumably at least partially due to the effects of COVID-19. As a result, only 11% of medium and large enterprises reported using digital technologies in 2020, and while no data are available for SMEs, OECD interviews suggest that the numbers could be even lower for the latter (National Statistics Office, 2022[23]).

Figure 4.2. Internet use of firms, and quality of available networks

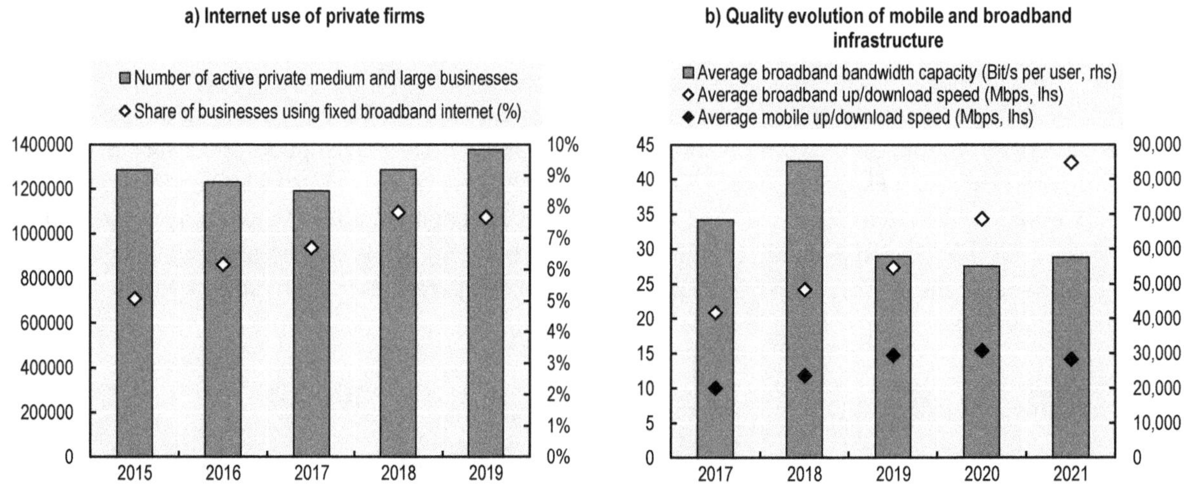

Note: In 2021, fixed broadband average speed stood at 55 for upper-middle income countries, and 113 for high-income countries, while the mobile broadband average speed stood at 25 and 51 respectively.
Source: (DAMU, 2020[24]) (Bureau of National Statistics, 2022[25]) (EIU, 2022[19]; ITU, 2022[20])

In Kazakhstan, as in many OECD countries, there is a persistent coverage gap between urban and small urban and rural areas. Narrowing this gap is critical to strengthening the overall economic development of these regions and the competitiveness of their small firms and entrepreneurs. Since the "last-mile" connectivity initiative has not yet been successful in connecting these regions, their municipal or regional governments, in co-operation with local interest groups and citizen-led initiatives could facilitate, build, operate or finance high-speed networks, compensating for the absence of operators. Across the OECD area, such municipal networks have been successful in extending connectivity in regions where deployment by national communication companies was lacking or deemed unprofitable; they have contributed to increased competition, and therefore lower prices, in areas where coverage was partially provided by national operators (Mölleryd, 2015[26]) (However, institutional framework conditions, in particular open competition in the telecom market, have proved an important enabler of such bottom-up initiatives in OECD countries such as Mexico, Sweden, the UK, and the US (OECD, 2021[27]).

4.3.1. Supporting firm-level digital uptake: the challenge of raising investment and modernising the regulatory framework

One clear trend in Kazakhstan that has significant implications for the digital transition is underinvestment in ICTs. Investment in ICTs in Kazakhstan amounted to only 1.98% of total GFCF, putting the country slightly ahead of Uzbekistan but significantly below the OECD average of 11.4%, and further still behind the leading OECD members Sweden (20%) and the Czech Republic (17%) (Figure 4.3). Relative to the size of the economy, the level is similarly low (equivalent to 0.46% GDP), comparable only to Poland among OECD members (0.78% GDP), and significantly behind the OECD average of 2.58% of GDP.

Figure 4.3. Investment in ICTs: Kazakhstan in international context

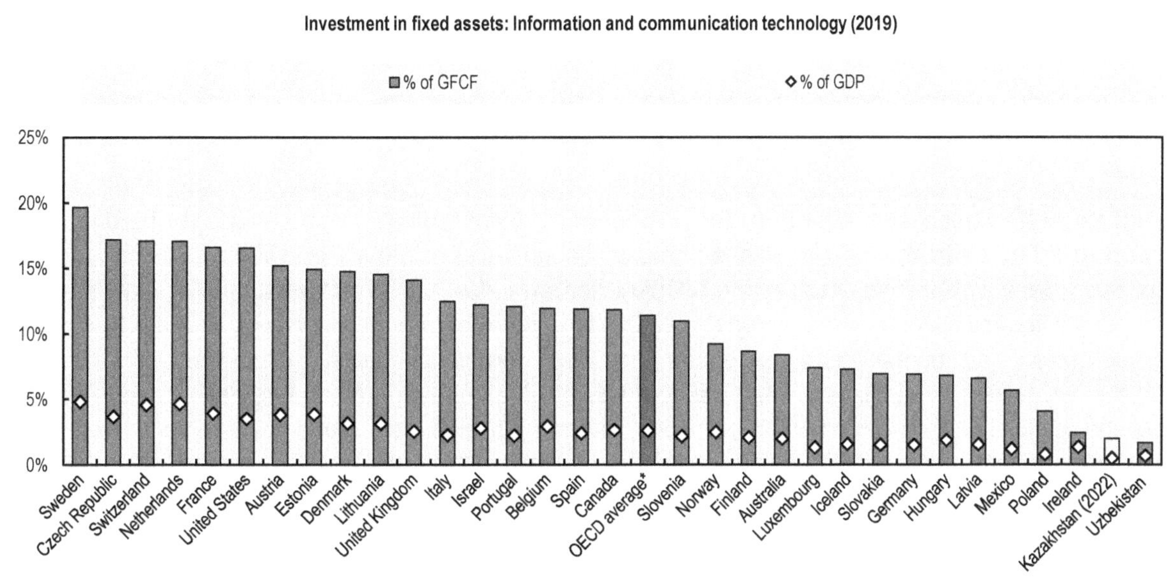

Note: *The OECD average does not include Chile, Colombia, Costa Rica, Greece, Japan, Korea, New Zealand.
Source: (OECD, 2023[28])

Raising the level of investment in ICTs and connectivity infrastructure is crucial for Kazakhstan to succeed in the digital transition. it is imperative that government strive to increase both the relative share and total volume of investment in these assets if its firms and workers are to be able to take advantage of the digital transformation, ensuring that the productivity and output of the country's private sector does not further diverge from the OECD average.

In recent years, Kazakhstan has worked to adapt the legal and policy framework for firms to new digital challenges. On the data front in particular, Kazakhstan has been regularly amending its legal framework to gradually move toward the privacy and security standards set by the European Union's General Data Protection Regulation (GDPR) (Government of Kazakhstan, 2013[29]; Government of Kazakhstan, 2017[30]). As part of these efforts, the government created the Information Security Committee under the MDDIAI, mandated with the implementation and monitoring of compliance with the Law on Data Protection (Government of Kazkahstan, 2022[31]). Though the objective was to create a Data Protection Agency following the GDPR model, the Committee's mandate so far focuses mostly on technological solutions to data issues, rather than on legislative and implementation aspects for data protection issues (CAISS, 2020[32]). The new legislative framework also imposes obligations on companies to appoint a data protection officer to ensure internal compliance with the Law, notify the Committee about data breaches, and carry out data protection impact assessments before engaging in any activity requiring the collection and handling of data (Dentons, 2021[33]).

One of the main areas for improvement highlighted by survey respondents was the need for better digital security (45% of respondents), which has been a policy priority for the government in recent years. As part of the country's broader digitalisation programme, the government has, for example, been developing digital security policies to reduce vulnerabilities to cyber threats (Government of Kazakhstan, 2017[34]). In 2016, the government launched the Cybersecurity Concept until 2022 ("Cyber Shield of Kazakhstan"), which aimed to develop a cybersecurity sector in the country, something that had previously been largely underdeveloped (Government of Kazakhstan, 2017[35]). The strategy included a number of important initial steps: (i) the creation of a national register of trusted digital software and IT products to reduce reliance on foreign solutions; (ii) enhanced international co-operation with internationally recognised private digital security providers and international organisations active in the domain to build local capacity; and (iii) the development of a digital culture for the general population and the training of cybersecurity specialists. Some of the targets of the initiative were further included in the objectives of the Digital Kazakhstan programme. In 2022, the government announced the launch of the Cybershield 2.0 programme, incorporating new challenges and aspects of the digital transformation in Kazakhstan, especially on the liberalisation and inclusion of the private sector, law enforcement, security, and defence sectors (OECD, 2023[3]).

The strategy has been successful so far in beginning to establish a cyber-security landscape in the country. On the institutional front, the National Security Council, the Council for Cybersecurity, the Information Security Committee under the MDDIAI and an industry information security centre covering the country's financial sector were created (ITU, 2021[36]). However, recent analysis by the OECD suggests that the current institutional architecture can lead to co-ordination issues, while businesses remain insufficiently aware of the initiatives implemented (OECD, 2023[3]). Kazakhstan has been actively seeking to expand international co-operation, in particular with the International Telecommunication Union (ITU), and through its involvement in the fourth industrial revolution working group of the World Economic Forum (WEF).

4.4. Equipping the private sector with skills for the digital transition remains a key policy challenge for the government

Ensuring that firms have the skills and knowledge needed to make the most of digitalisation is crucial for both competitiveness and inclusion. The ability of private sector firms to make the most of the opportunities presented by the digitalisation transition, and to ensure that they are not left behind by competitors both domestically and internationally, depends on the capacities of firms to use a range of digital technologies, as well as complementary capacities in other areas necessary to identify commercial or organisational use cases for those same technologies too (such as management skills that reflect how digitalisation can affect firm organisation).

For example, the ability of a manufacturing SME to innovate with respect to their internal organisation or production depends on their ability to derive new data and insights from data using digital tools. It is for this reason that, in a study on the impact of various policy interventions and framework conditions on the diffusion of digital technologies in the EU, the OECD found that the intervention with the greatest single impact was upgrading technical and managerial skills of firms (Figure 4.4) At the same time, firms must have the internal capacities and knowledge to recognise the *value* of using digital tools for their business, and to have the skills necessary to recognise opportunities where digitalisation would be of use to them.

Figure 4.4. Impact of selected policy interventions on improving productivity

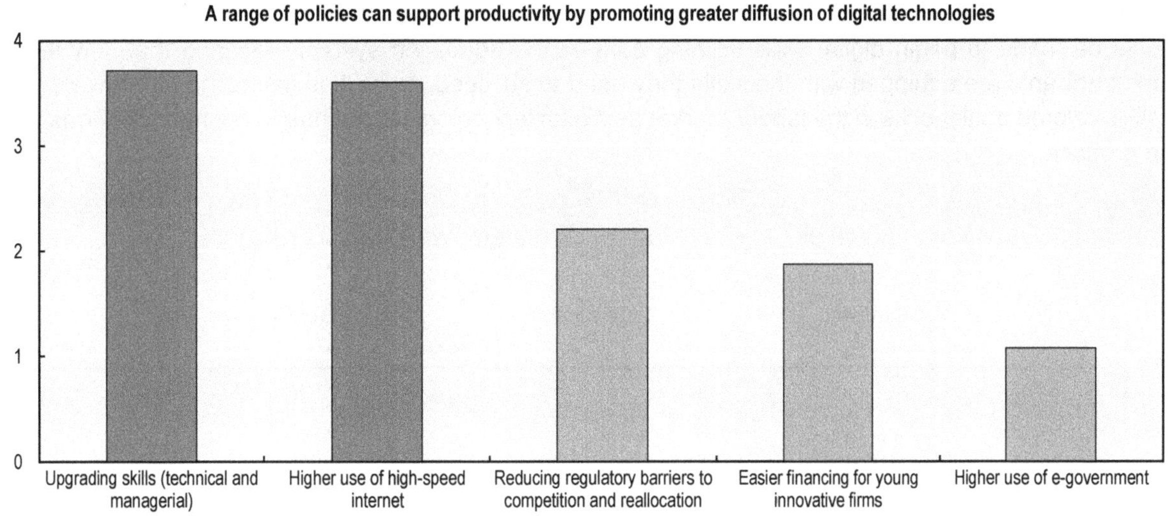

Note: Effect on multifactor productivity of the average EU firm of closing half of the gap with best-performing EU countries in a range of structural and policy areas, after 3 years
Source: (OECD, 2019[37])

The type of skills that the workforce needs to make the most of the digital transition are manifold. In certain cases, new types of jobs and the changing nature of existing ones require job holders to have a mix of technical and high-level cognitive skills, for example, database management skills and related data analytical skills. In some professions, for example, there may develop a need for proficiency in coding languages such as Python and Java, or knowledge of and experience with machine learning, data science and visualisation. These are advanced skills, ones which are not widely held even in OECD countries (1% of workforce), but they are nevertheless important for Kazakhstan and other transition economies if they are not to be left behind by new forms of value creation, drivers of productivity, and innovation (OECD, 2022[38]). At the same time, more "basic" skills, such as a familiarity with widely used software or experience with social media platforms are increasingly important to a wide range of industries, beyond the traditional confines of the ICT sector. Whilst there are, of course, sector- and industry-specific digital skills needs, the whole-of-economy significance of digitalisation requires an inclusive approach to digital skills development.

While it is clear that digitalisation offers significant opportunities for innovation and productivity growth for Kazakhstan's SMEs, the uneven diffusion of infrastructure and skills risks aggregating productivity gaps between firms due to difficulties in financing digital technologies and the related intangible capital necessary to use them effectively. Access to finance challenges are long-standing barriers to firm growth in Kazakhstan, in part due to the pervasive presence of the state in the banking sector and issues relating to preferential SOE lending. The banking sector's stringent collateral requirements are particularly difficult for SMEs in the digital context, where much investment is in intangible capital (skills, software and other forms of intellectual property). Ensuring a broad access to the skills and capacities necessary to make the most of digitalisation is therefore also important for inclusion, be it at the industrial level (i.e., between firms and industries with more or less investment capacity), regional level (i.e., between SMEs in Almaty and major industrial hubs and more rural areas of the country), or socio-economic level (i.e., gendered differences in terms of access to digital skills).

The level of digital skills in Kazakhstan has still to catch up with the OECD average, though it is notably higher than in Uzbekistan and other regional peers (Figure 4.5); less than 30% of the population have basic ICT skills, which is half the OECD average. This is true across the basic, standard, and advanced skills categories, suggesting that the labour force in Kazakhstan remains underequipped to use even the more basic of digital technologies and to recognise potential applications for them in their own businesses, or indeed in the context of a start-up or innovation. Raising the general level of digital skills should be a priority for the government in their pursuit of private sector competitiveness, and efforts should be made to begin digital skills training early in the education system, ensuring that new labour market entrants are equipped with the skills they need to succeed, as well as mitigating the development of skills-related bottlenecks in the labour market as digital technologies continue to change how firms work and produce.

Figure 4.5. Overview of digital skills: Kazakhstan, Uzbekistan and OECD average

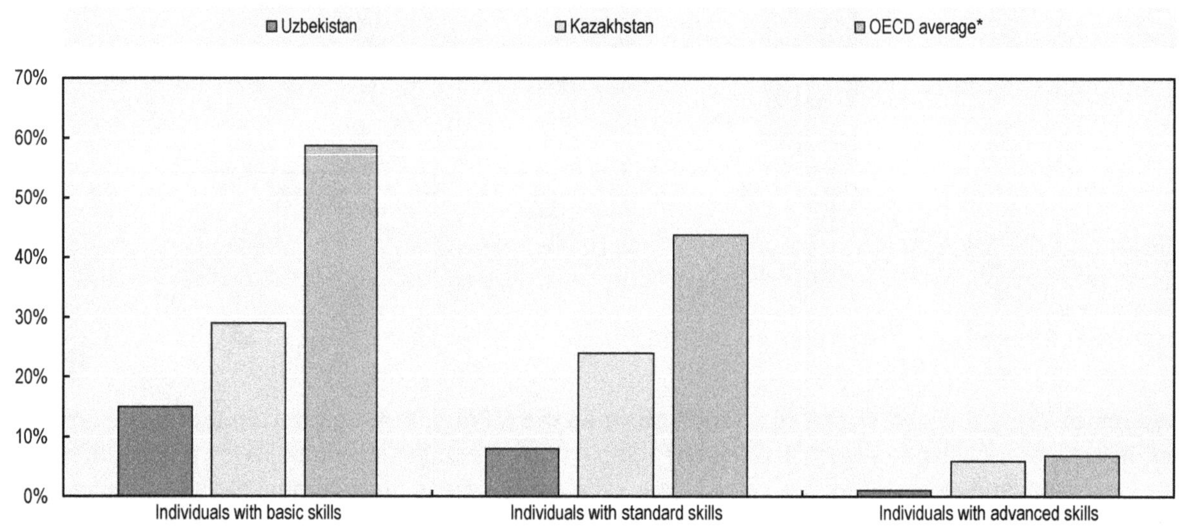

Note: As a percentage of the population. *Data was not available for Australia, Canada, Costa Rica, Israel, New Zealand, United States. Data for Uzbekistan is from 2018-2020, data for Kazakhstan is from 2019-2020. Observations for OECD countries go from 2013 to 2020. Data for Uzbekistan used as a comparator for Kazakhstan due to data availability.
Source: (ITU, 2023[18])

The difference in digital skills levels in Kazakhstan and peer countries is less stark in the areas that are likely to be productivity enhancing, i.e., where the person uses their digital knowledge to create new knowledge and insights from data, or to innovate and improve communications (WEF, 2020[39]) (OECD, 2021[40]). For example, around a quarter of Kazakhstan's population have standard digital skills, meaning that they have experience in tasks such as using an arithmetic formula in a spreadsheet, creating an electronic presentation, connecting new electronic devices, or downloading and configuring software (Figure 4.6). In advanced skills, which include tasks such as programming, Kazakhstan is close to the OECD average. Greater data availability on digital skills and digital diffusion in the business community, for example in terms of firm size and industry, would allow for more targeted policy interventions should they be necessary.

Figure 4.6. Breakdown of digital skills: Kazakhstan, Uzbekistan and the OECD average (2019)

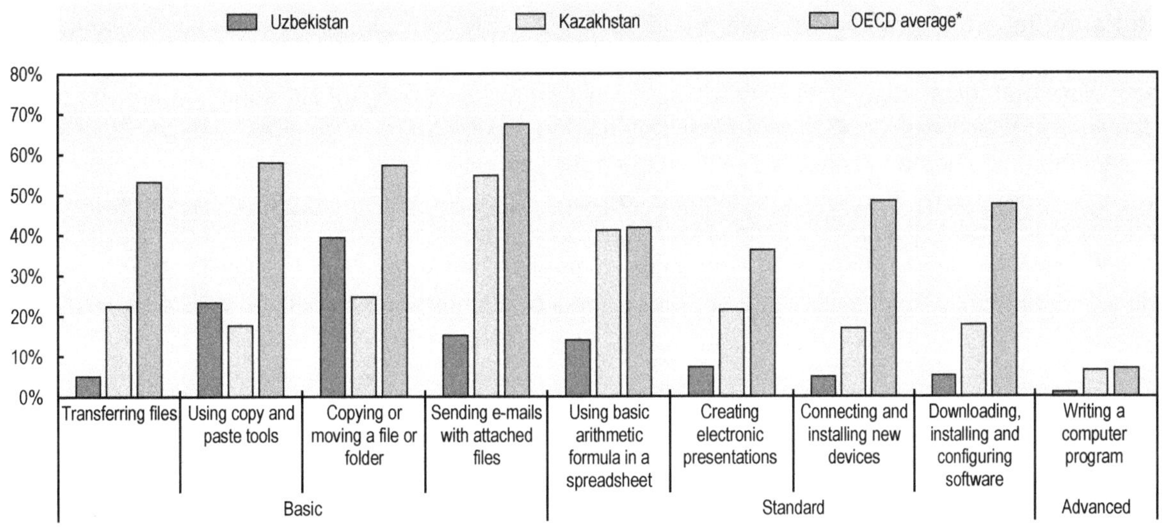

Note: As a percentage of the population. *Data was not available for Australia, Canada, Costa Rica, Israel, New Zealand, United States. Data for Uzbekistan is from 2018-2020, data for Kazakhstan is from 2019-2020. Observations for OECD countries go from 2013 to 2020.
Source: (ITU, 2023[18])

One characteristic of the digital skills landscape in Kazakhstan, as in Uzbekistan, is that the digital skills gap is relatively ungendered. The gap between men and women in basic, standard and advanced skills is significantly higher in the OECD than it is in Kazakhstan and Uzbekistan (Figure 4.7). Given the generally low level of digital skills in the country, the relatively narrow gender gap may be more representative of the broader availability of these skills rather than a positive trend in their development. Nevertheless, the government has an opportunity to ensure that the policy interventions to develop digital skills build on rather than diverge from the relatively ungendered dispersal of digital skills that the country currently has.

Figure 4.7. Gender differences in the digital skills gap: Kazakhstan, Uzbekistan and the OECD average (2019, in percentage points)

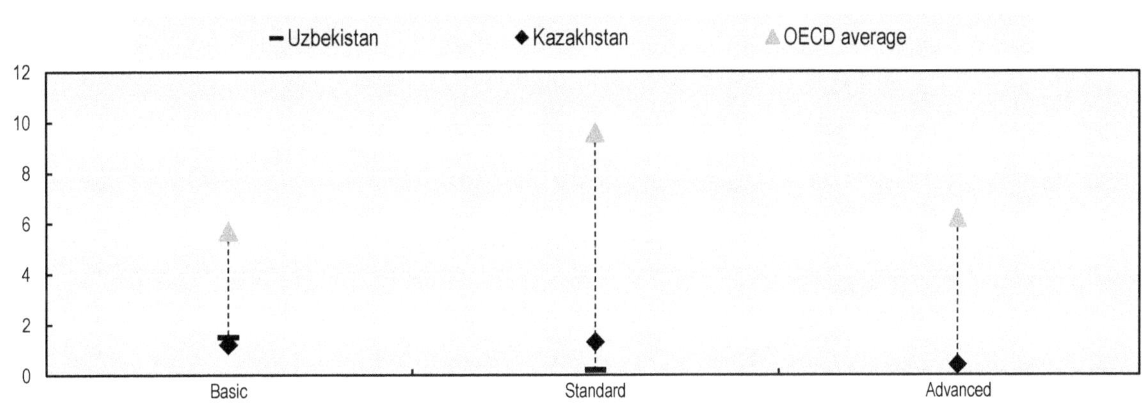

Note: As a percentage of the population. OECD estimations based on ITU data. Data was not available for Australia, Canada, Costa Rica, Israel, New Zealand, United States. Data for Uzbekistan is from 2018-2020, data for Kazakhstan is from 2019-2020. Observations for OECD countries go from 2013 to 2020.
Source: (ITU, 2023[18])

It is important to note that a country's historically important industries can create path dependencies in skills availability and development that can either enable or inhibit the private sector's digital – and green – transition (OECD, 2022[41]). If, for example, in a certain economy there has been a historically high importance of a given sector or industry where gender gaps are present, then it may follow that the starting point from which to inclusively develop digital skills may be uneven (e.g., if an industry in which digitalisation has clear potential to increase productivity and innovation, such as manufacturing, has had a historically significant gender gap in terms of employment or productivity, then there may be structural barriers to overcome to ensure that the development of digital skills is truly inclusive). One of the key policy challenges for Kazakhstan is therefore in ensuring that pre-existing gender gaps in terms of employment generally or access to high-productivity employment specifically (for example, in manufacturing) do not act as de facto barriers to the inclusion of women in digital skills development.

References

Bureau of National Statistics (2022), *Small and Medium Enterprises (database)*, https://stat.gov.kz/official/industry/139/statistic/6 (accessed on 29 April 2022). [25]

Cable (2022), *Worldwide mobile data pricing 2021*, https://www.cable.co.uk/mobiles/worldwide-data-pricing/ (accessed on 28 April 2022). [17]

CAISS (2020), *Protection of personal data in Kazakhstan: status, risks and opportunities (Защита персональных данных в Казахстане: статус, риски и возможности)*, https://www.soros.kz/wp-content/uploads/2020/04/Personal_data_report.pdf. [32]

DAMU (2020), *Annual Report on SMEs Development in Kazakhstan and its regions*, https://damu.kz/upload/iblock/192/Damu_Book_2019_EN.pdf. [24]

Dentons (2021), *The impact of the GDPR in Kazakhstan*, https://www.dentons.com/en/insights/alerts/2021/may/5/the-impact-of-the-gdpr-in-kazakhstan. [33]

Digital Kazakhstan (2022), *About the Program*, https://digitalkz.kz/en/about-the-program/ (accessed on 17 May 2022). [7]

egov.kz (2021), *"Informational Kazakhstan – 2020" State program*, https://egov.kz/cms/en/articles/gp_inf_kaz_2020 (accessed on 17 May 2022). [6]

EIU (2022), *The Inclusive Internet Index (database)*, https://theinclusiveinternet.eiu.com/ (accessed on 21 April 2022). [19]

Government of Kazakhstan (2022), *Regular meeting of Commission on Demonopolization of Economy under Government of Kazakhstan took place*, https://primeminister.kz/en/news/kr-ukimeti-zhanyndagy-ekonomikany-demonopolizaciyalau-zhonindegi-komissiyanyn-kezekti-otyrysy-otti-531719 (accessed on 5 July 2022). [14]

Government of Kazakhstan (2021), *Digital Era Lifestyle Programme*. [10]

Government of Kazakhstan (2017), *Approval of the Cybersecurity Concept ("Cyber Shield of Kazakhstan"), Resolution by the Government of the Republic of Kazakhstan No. 407*, https://adilet.zan.kz/rus/docs/P1700000407 (accessed on 31 May 2022). [35]

Government of Kazakhstan (2017), *Law "On Amendments and Additions to Certain Legislative Acts of the Republic of Kazakhstan on Regulation of Digital Technologies", 25 June 2020*, https://adilet.zan.kz/eng/docs/Z1700000051 (accessed on 6 July 2022). [30]

Government of Kazakhstan (2017), *State of the Nation Address*, https://www.akorda.kz/en/addresses/addresses_of_president/the-president-of-kazakhstan-nursultan-nazarbayevs-address-to-the-nation-of-kazakhstan-january-31-2017 (accessed on 13 July 2022). [34]

Government of Kazakhstan (2017), *State programme "Digital Kazakhstan:*, https://digitalkz.kz/wp-content/uploads/2020/03/%D0%93%D0%9F%20%D0%A6%D0%9A%20%D0%BD%D0%B0%20%D0%B0%D0%BD%D0%B3%D0%BB%2003,06,2020.pdf. [5]

Government of Kazakhstan (2014), *Government Decree No. 280 of 31 March 2014 ('On approval of the Comprehensive Privatisation Plan for 2014-2016'*, https://www.skc.kz/upload/iblock/ffe/ii.-postanovlenie-pravitelstva-rk-ot-31-03-2014-_-280.pdf. [12]

Government of Kazakhstan (2013), *Law of the Republic of Kazakhstan dated 21 May 2013 On personal data and their protection*, https://adilet.zan.kz/eng/docs/Z1300000094#:~:text=The%20Law%20of%20the%20Republic,94%2DV.&text=This%20Law%20regulates%20the%20public,and%20protection%20of%20personal%20data. (accessed on 7 July 2022). [29]

Government of Kazkahstan (2022), *Information Security Committee under the Ministry of Digital Development, Innovation and Aerospace Industry*, https://www.gov.kz/memleket/entities/infsecurity/activities/directions?lang=en (accessed on 12 July 2022). [31]

ITU (2023), *ITU Digital Development Dashboard*, ITU, World Telecommunication/ICT Indicators Database, https://www.itu.int/en/ITU-D/Statistics/Dashboards/Pages/Digital-Development.aspx. [18]

ITU (2022), *Digital Development (database)*, http://itu.int (accessed on 27 April 2022). [15]

ITU (2022), *World Telecommunication/ICT Indicators Database online*, https://www.itu.int/pub/D-IND-WTID.OL-2021/fr (accessed on 29 April 2022). [20]

ITU (2021), *How Kazakhstan Efficiently Implements Its National Cybersecurity Strategy*, https://www.itu.int/en/ITU-D/Regional-Presence/CIS/Pages/News/20210810.aspx (accessed on 1 June 2022). [36]

ITU (2021), *The affordability of ICT services 2020*, https://www.itu.int/en/ITU-D/Statistics/Documents/publications/prices2020/ITU_A4AI_Price_Briefing_2020.pdf. [16]

Kazinform (2015), *"TransTeleCom" JSC sold within privatization programme*, https://strategy2050.kz/en/news/21462/ (accessed on 7 July 2022). [13]

Mölleryd, B. (2015), "Development of High-speed Networks and the Role of Municipal Networks", *OECD Science, Technology and Industry Policy Papers*, No. 26, OECD Publishing, Paris, https://doi.org/10.1787/5jrqdl7rvns3-en. [26]

National Statistics Office (2022), *Share of large and medium-sized industrial enterprises using digital technologies (database)*, https://stat.gov.kz/api/getFile/?docId=ESTAT410029 (accessed on 3 May 2022). [23]

OECD (2023), *Digital Kazakhstan Government Programme*, OECD STIP Compass, OECD Publishing, https://stip.oecd.org/stip/interactive-dashboards/policy-initiatives/2021%2Fdata%2FpolicyInitiatives%2F25280. [2]

OECD (2023), *Digital Skills for Private Sector Competitiveness*, OECD Publishing, Paris. [4]

OECD (2023), *Improving Framework Conditions for the Digital Transformation of Businesses: Peer review of Kazakhstan*, OECD Publishing, Paris. [3]

OECD (2023), *Investment by asset (indicator)*, https://doi.org/10.1787/8e5d47e6-en. [28]

OECD (2022), *OECD Reviews of Innovation Policy: Germany 2022: Building Agility for Successful Transitions*, OECD Reviews of Innovation Policy, OECD Publishing, Paris, https://doi.org/10.1787/50b32331-en. [41]

OECD (2022), *Skills for the Digital Transition: Assessing Recent Trends using Big Data*, OECD Publishing, Paris, https://www.oecd-ilibrary.org/docserver/38c36777-en.pdf?expires=1676976769&id=id&accname=ocid84004878&checksum=5BF20BE13D076B519F8C025F7ADC90E8. [38]

OECD (2021), *Bridging digital divides in G20 countries*, OECD Publishing, Paris, https://doi.org/10.1787/35c1d850-en. [27]

OECD (2021), *OECD Skills Outlook 2021: Learning for Life*, OECD Publishing, Paris, https://www.oecd-ilibrary.org/docserver/0ae365b4-en.pdf?expires=1681746986&id=id&accname=ocid84004878&checksum=50264747 5D6197768ACBA081E248F600. [40]

OECD (2021), *The Digital Transformation of SMEs*, OECD Studies on SMEs and Entrepreurship, OECD Publishing, Paris, https://www.oecd-ilibrary.org/docserver/bdb9256a-en.pdf?expires=1681399065&id=id&accname=ocid84004878&checksum=A2E2D7459BF4010808A59FFA2267BADA. [1]

OECD (2019), *Digitalisation and productivity: A story of complementarities*, OECD Economic Outlook: 2019, https://www.oecd-ilibrary.org/sites/b2e897b0-en/1/2/2/index.html?itemId=/content/publication/b2e897b0-en&_csp_=d2743ede274dd564946a04fc1f43d5dc&itemIGO=oecd&itemContentType=book. [37]

OECD (n.d.), *OECD Studies on SMEs and Entrepreneurship*, OECD Publishing, Paris, https://doi.org/10.1787/20780990. [21]

Republic of Kazakhstan (2022), *DigitEL | Digital Era Lifestyle*. [8]

Samruk Kazyna (2016), *Telecommunications industry - transformation of the industry*, https://www.sk.kz/upload/iblock/203/203b9191c8d1418e26398339be71f90b.pdf. [11]

United Nations (2022), *UN E-Government Knowledgease*, United Nations, NYC, https://publicadministration.un.org/egovkb/en-us/Data/Country-Information/id/87-Kazakhstan. [9]

WEF (2020), *The Future of Jobs Report 2020*, WEF, Geneva, https://www.weforum.org/reports/the-future-of-jobs-report-2020. [39]

World Bank (2021), *World Bank Enterprise Survey*. [22]

Notes

[1] At the time of writing, a new draft law is under consideration to increase the liabilities of the operators in case of low or deteriorating network quality.

[2] The term "connectivity gap" refers to gaps in access and uptake of high-quality broadband services at affordable prices in areas with low population densities and for disadvantaged groups compared to the population as a whole (OECD, 2021[27]).

5 Improving the operational environment for firms: focus on trade facilitation and contract enforcement

In recent years, the government has made significant progress in improving the ease and reliability of the *de jure* and *de facto* conditions in which firms conduct their business and manage their interactions with public bodies. Responses to the survey suggest that while the business community feels generally positive about the business environment in Kazakhstan, there are issues that continue to affect their operations, and in turn which may mitigate government efforts to diversify its economy. Building on survey insights, this chapter focusses on two such issues: trade facilitation and contract enforcement.

5.1. Survey observations and overview

Responses to the survey indicated that firms were largely positive on the progress of numerous reforms to support the business climate. Respondents overwhelmingly reported that many aspects of the regulatory and policy environment that affect their daily operations are conducive to doing business and had improved over recent years. This positive assessment reflects the significant efforts that the government has made in recent years to reform these areas. This is true both in terms of operational reforms, such as expanded service delivery through digitalisation, as well as in terms of legal clarity, for example through the introduction of the 2015 Entrepreneurial Code of Kazakhstan in 2015, and the Environmental Code in 2021.

The generally high level of positivity for the direction of reforms was reflected in a broad optimism and enthusiasm for doing business in Kazakhstan. Only 6% of respondents considered the business climate to be unfriendly, whereas 23% of respondents reported that it was very friendly, with another 68% describing it as somewhat friendly.[1] Respondents also noted their commitment to Kazakhstan despite uncertainty in the external environment due to Russia's war of aggression in Ukraine and the disruptions causes by the COVID-19 pandemic; almost half of respondents expected to see an increase in profits and trade turnover in 2022 (48% and 42% respectively). The picture that emerges from respondents is therefore of a country where doing business is becoming easier, and where doing so is increasingly attractive.

At the same time, praise for reform progress was not uniform, and survey responses indicates concerns with a number of policy areas that may particularly affect the operations of local SMEs. Issues faced by SMEs are a bellwether for the business climate more broadly; if a local firm faces challenges in diversifying its production due to cumbersome customs arrangements, or to settling disputes with other firms or public bodies due to inefficient contract enforcement, then the implications are significant for any foreign or domestic investor entering or considering entry into the market. It is therefore vital that the government sees the barriers faced in the day-to-day running of a local business as being deeply intertwined with the success of other policy agendas, such as attracting investment into non-oil sectors of the economy and supporting the diversification and competitiveness of Kazakhstan in the green and digital transitions.

Building on insights from the survey, this chapter focusses on two policy areas that are important for private sector development and diversification in Kazakhstan: customs policy and contract enforcement. These are crucial if domestic firms are to have the confidence to invest and contribute to the country's diversification agenda, but they also give international investors confidence in the ability of the local private and public sector to play a role in their value chains and be predictable clients.

5.1.1. Reforms have made doing business in Kazakhstan significantly easier, but harder-to-tackle challenges continue to beset the business climate

A majority of firms rated each of the surveyed indicators as either very useful or somewhat useful. While the share of firms ranking most indicators as very useful was below 25%, very few firms indicated that they found the given policy area not useful. This was not a relative ranking, and firms were not asked to rate one policy area over another in terms of its utility for their business operations, but it does suggest that survey respondents broadly agreed with the direction of travel of policy intervention (Figure 5.1 a).

Respondent firms were most positive on reform progress to improve business registration and licensing, which may have contributed to easing bureaucratic constraints on doing business in the country. The only indicator where a clear majority of respondents rated progress in a given policy area strongly was registration and licensing measures (63% of respondents reported reforms to the registration and licensing framework as very useful, with a further 22% rating them somewhat useful). To a certain extent, these reforms involved the rationalisation and simplification of the procedures and costs required for doing business in Kazakhstan. These reforms were therefore very important to establishing a more attractive operational environment, but they were also, in the context of limited progress in other areas of pro-competition and pro-market reforms, relatively easy to implement.

A large majority of firms thought that either major or a certain amount of progress had been made in almost all of the local business climate indicators over the past five years. The most significant areas of progress were linked to areas that involved a technological or digital component: improvements in digital infrastructure, access to new technologies, and the digitally driven improvements in business and licensing procedures (Figure 5.1 b). With the exception of taxation, a majority of respondents deemed each surveyed reform area to be moving in the right direction, if at an uneven pace. Nevertheless, there was a significantly higher proportion of respondents who were either ambivalent or negative about reform progress than those who were positive. The positivity of respondents to reform progress in Kazakhstan was also markedly lower than responses to the survey in Uzbekistan, though this may in part reflect the particularly strong reform momentum with certain reforms to support the business climate taken by the government in Tashkent since 2017, as well as higher firm-level expectations of the Kazakh authorities due to the relative maturity of the reform process in the country.

Figure 5.1. Firm-level evaluation of the status of reforms in Kazakhstan

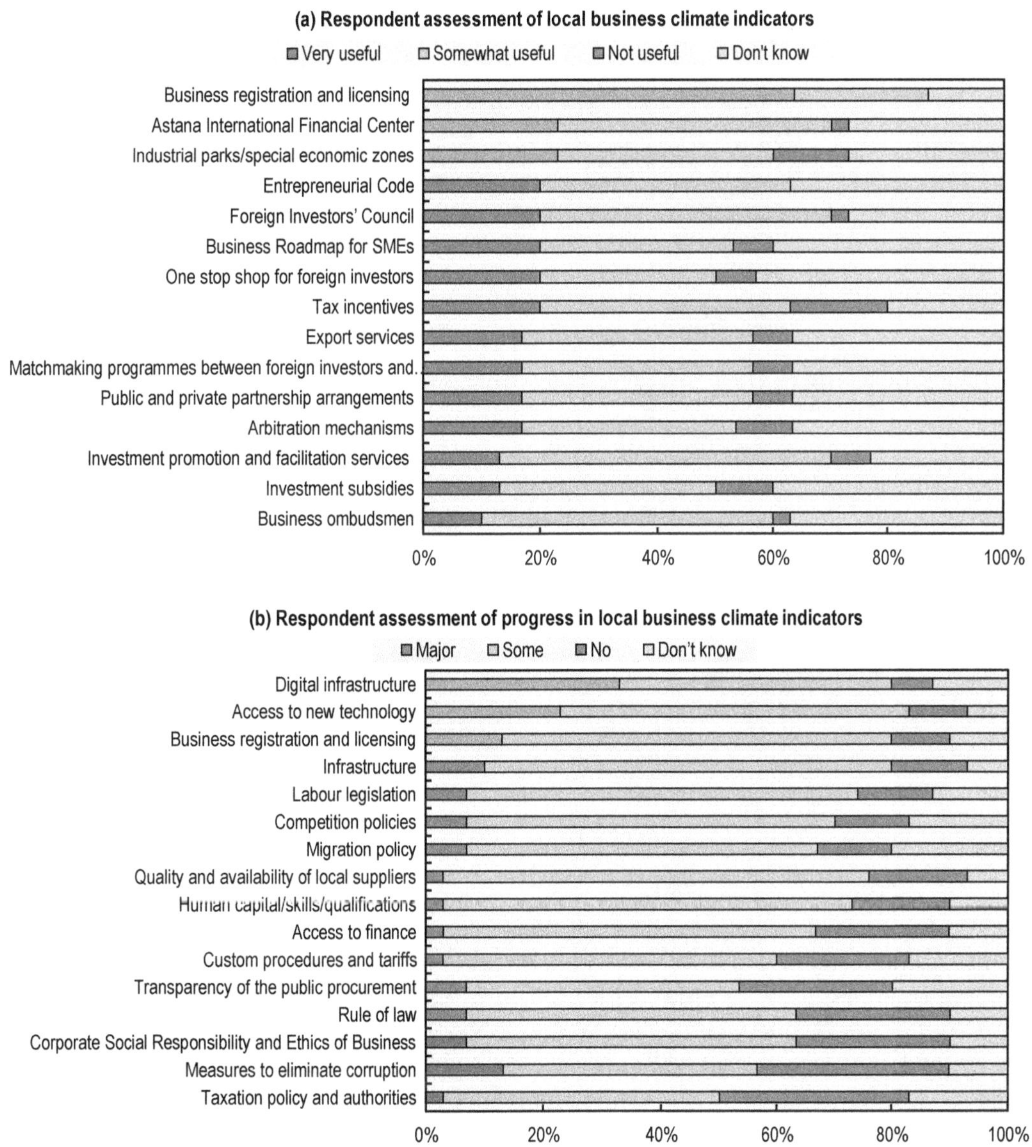

Note: As a percentage of the total number of respondents.
Source: EU-OECD Business Climate Assessment Survey in Kazakhstan

A sizeable plurality of firms reported limited progress with a number of key operational aspects of the local business climate, including customs procedures. Almost a quarter of respondents (23%) claimed that there had been no improvements to customs procedures and tariffs, with another 57% claiming only limited progress. These two issues highlight the persistent challenge that the government faces in ensuring that *de jure* improvements to the business climate are properly implemented, since, for example, the country has in fact made relatively strong progress in OECD assessments of customs and trade policies, such as the OECD Trade Facilitation Indicators. That the *de jure* progress in these areas has not been felt in the *de facto* operations of respondents in Kazakhstan indicates that on the ground implementation remains challenging for the authorities.

The two biggest weaknesses of the business climate were reported to be bureaucracy and corruption. These are transversal issues, affecting a wide variety of policy areas, but they are strongly relevant to the issues of customs procedures and contract enforcement, where previous OECD work has highlighted how corruption, bureaucracy and transparency issues can undermine the business environment (OECD, 2021[1]). Rather than being separate issues to be treated independently, bureaucracy and corruption can instead be both the drivers and symptoms of the challenges faced by firms in different policy areas, including trade and contract enforcement.

Figure 5.2. Challenges in the business climate and priority reforms

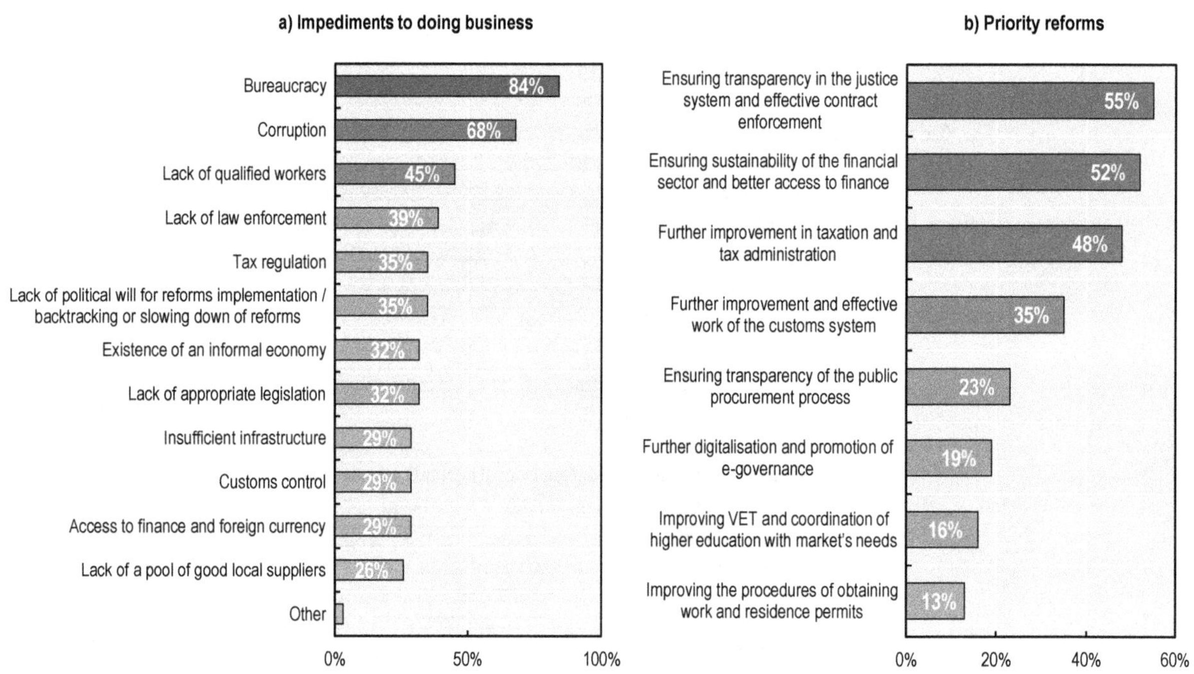

Note: As a percentage of the total number of respondents.
Source: EU-OECD Business Climate Assessment Survey in Kazakhstan

Respondents considered reforms to improve contract enforcement to be the most important area for action the government to consider. When asked which reforms they considered most important for the government to pursue, over half of respondents suggested reforms to improve transparency in the justice system and effective contract enforcement (55%) and improving the health of the financial sector and access to finance (52%). A significant proportion of respondents suggested reforms to the tax administration (48%) and the customs system (35%).

5.2. Supporting firm internationalisation through trade facilitation and customs reform

Kazakhstan's government has long recognised the importance of international trade for the country's economy. Yet despite ambitions to deepen economic internationalisation, firms continue to face significant barriers in accessing international markets. In part this reflects questions of economic structure, since many of the country's SMEs are active in non-tradable sectors, and the productivity of those in tradable sectors is often insufficient to make them competitive internationally. Those that do or could trade abroad face higher distance penalties than competitors in many OECD countries, in part due to the vast distances that goods must travel to reach their destinations, but in part also to the ineffectiveness of the policies and regulations that govern trade, which raise the fixed costs associated with internationalising.

There is much that the government can do and is doing to improve physical infrastructure for trade, though these interventions often involve significant investment and raise complex questions of governance and sustainability. Yet as discussed in a joint OECD-ITF report on freight connectivity in Central Asia, a significant proportion of the connectivity penalty facing firms in the region is attributable neither to geography nor to physical infrastructure, but to policies, the "soft infrastructure" that dictates the movement of goods, services and people (ITF, 2019[2]).

The government has made significant efforts to improve the "soft connectivity" that shapes the country's international trade conditions. The country formalised its commitment to developing an open and fair regulatory framework for trade through its accession to the World Trade Organisation (WTO) in 2015, and has signalled its intention to deepen its work with the relevant substantive committees on trade and agriculture at the OECD. As of 2023, Kazakhstan was not yet fully compliant with its WTO accession requirements, having implemented 61% of WTO commitments (of which Cat. A: 44.5%, Cat. B 16.8%, Cat. C 0%), below the implementation level of Tajikistan (79.4%) and the Kyrgyz Republic (77.7%).[2]

The country has also deepened its integration into regional blocs. Kazakhstan's membership of the Eurasian Economic Union (EEU) and prior integration into the Eurasian Customs Union (Belarus-Kazakhstan-Russia), as well as its active membership in the Central Asia Regional Economic Cooperation (CAREC) could enhance intra- and inter-regional economic integration. As in other countries of the EEU, it is unclear how existing trade and investment agreements have been and will be reconciled with its treaty obligations, nor how the government will navigate any tensions arising from sanctions on Russia and their shared membership of these blocs. Nonetheless, 70% of respondents to the survey are in favour of a greater integration of Kazakhstan in international trade with the opening of new exportations routes, while the other 30% has either no opinion or doesn't know.

Major modernisation of the customs infrastructure has helped to simplify procedures for traders. The introduction of fully automated customs procedures and the harmonisation and digitisation of all customs- and trade-related documentation through the *Automated System of Customs and Tax Authorities* ASTANA-1, which is fully compliant with the WTO, European Union and UNCTAD Customs standards, in January 2020 have been important steps to bring down the time and cost of trade. Their effects on businesses will have to be assessed in the coming years. In the meantime, improved co-ordination between customs and the Risk Management System inspections could provide additional improvements by avoiding overlapping or artificially lengthy procedures.

Improvements to trade facilitation could further reduce costs for Kazakhstan's firms. Against the background of the country's landlocked location and the legacy of Russia-oriented hard infrastructure, significant connectivity improvements could be made through trade facilitation, in particular by improving the effectiveness of border crossing procedures and raising levels of intra-agency co-operation (ITF, 2019[2]). Despite significant improvements over time, Kazakhstan continues to underperform on customs and border procedures relative to OECD countries, which is reflected in the country's performance in the *OECD Trade Facilitation Indicators* (TFI). Poor trade facilitation arrangements serve to increase the "distance penalties" that producers in Kazakhstan already face as a result of their location and the constraints imposed by physical infrastructure bottlenecks.

Firms continue to complain of cumbersome trade procedures and their inconsistent implementation. Over a third of survey respondents claimed that improvements to trade and customs regulation should be a government priority, while only 3% said that major progress had been made in this area over the past five years, despite Kazakhstan's *de jure* improvement in this area. The gap between firm-level experience and the *de jure* framework for operations speaks to a persistent implementation gap, which undermines government ambitions to provide the private sector with greater clarity in international trade, and limits the effectiveness of measures aimed at improving the ability of the local private sector to be competitive abroad.

5.2.1. Kazakhstan's performance in the OECD TFIs suggests indicates an improved trade facilitation framework in recent years

In the 2022 edition of the OECD TFIs, the OECD found that Kazakhstan had improved its performance in almost all areas covered by the indicators since the previous assessment in 2017. Particular progress was seen in improving the transparency and predictability of trade-related information, the streamlining of documentation requirements and processes, including an increased use of digital tools, and improving internal border agency co-operation (Figure 5.3)

Figure 5.3. Kazakhstan: Progress 2017-22 in the OECD TFIs

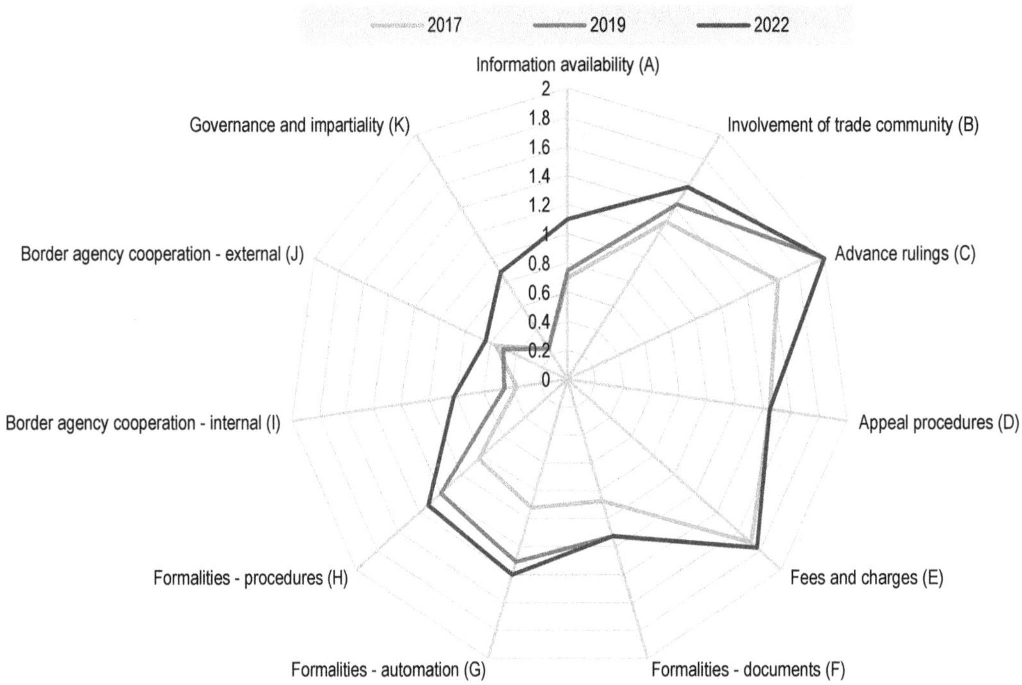

Source: (OECD, 2023[3])

Improvements in the overall TFI indicators have been driven by changes in particular policy areas. The improvements to the availability of trade-related information result from the country making more information available on its trade agreements and appeal procedures, by improving the operation of its enquiry points, and publishing user manuals on new systems that have been implemented. Guidelines and procedures that govern public consultation processes have also been developed, and the government is increasingly looking to involve the trade community in the design and day-to-day operation of border-related policies and procedures, with drafts of new changes also increasingly made available before entering into force. Progress has also been made regarding the publication of rules applicable to advance rulings, the opportunity to receive an advance ruling, and the publication of advance rulings that are of a general interest.

As in other areas of public service delivery, the government has also made significant progress in using digitalisation to streamline documentation and process requirements. Since 2017, the authorities have increasingly accepted copies of trade-related documents rather than originals, and they have also reduced the number and complexity of the documents required for foreign trade. Much of this progress is attributable to increased use of automation tools, which has improved pre-arrival processing possibilities (the ability to lodge trade documents in advance in an electronic format, including through a digital single window).

Internal and external border co-operation was one of the major areas for improvement highlighted in earlier versions of the OECD TFIs as well as a 2021 OECD report (OECD, 2021[1]). Here too the government has made notable progress, due in part to increased levels of coordination and harmonisation of data requirements and documentary controls among agencies involved in the management of cross-border trade. This has been complemented by increased real time availability of relevant data among domestic agencies, and in setting a clear basis for the coordination of risk management systems implemented by various agencies, including the shared results of inspections and controls.

Figure 5.4. Kazakhstan: OECD TFI performance in global context

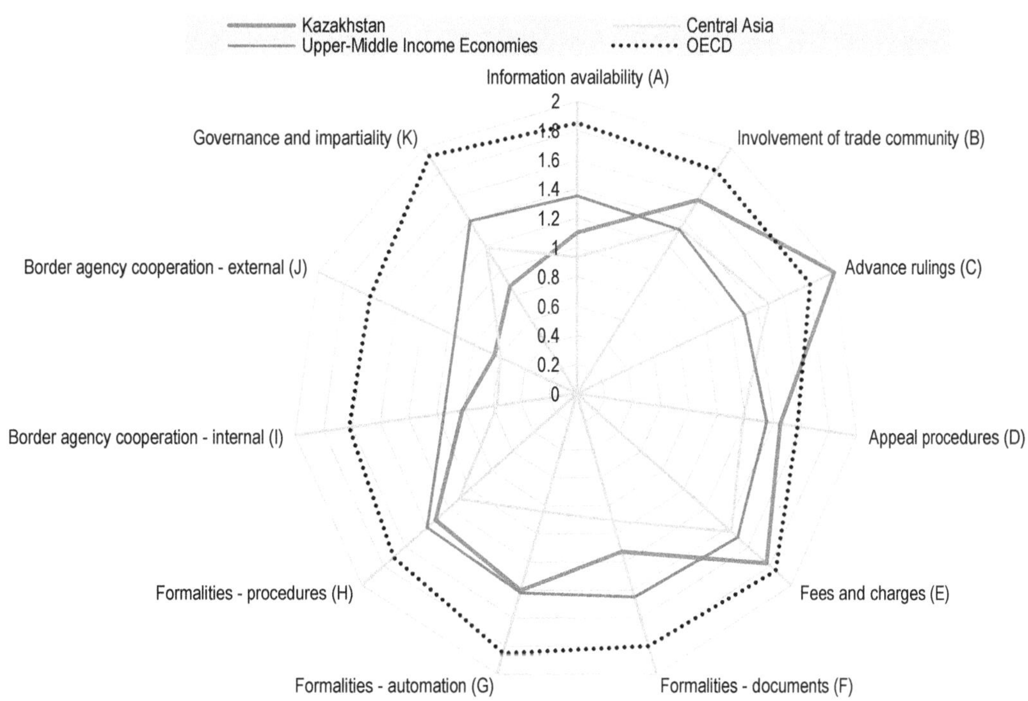

Source: (OECD, 2023[3])

Kazakhstan's performance in an international context demonstrates that the country still has significant scope to cut the cost of trade through additional customs reform and simplification. Nevertheless, while Kazakhstan performs relatively well in comparison to other upper-middle income countries, it continues to lag the OECD average in most areas covered by the indicators (Figure 5.4 .

Kazakhstan is Central Asia's top performer on each of the indicators with the exception of the governance and impartiality of customs procedures (Figure 5.5)

Figure 5.5. Kazakhstan: OECD TFI performance in a regional context

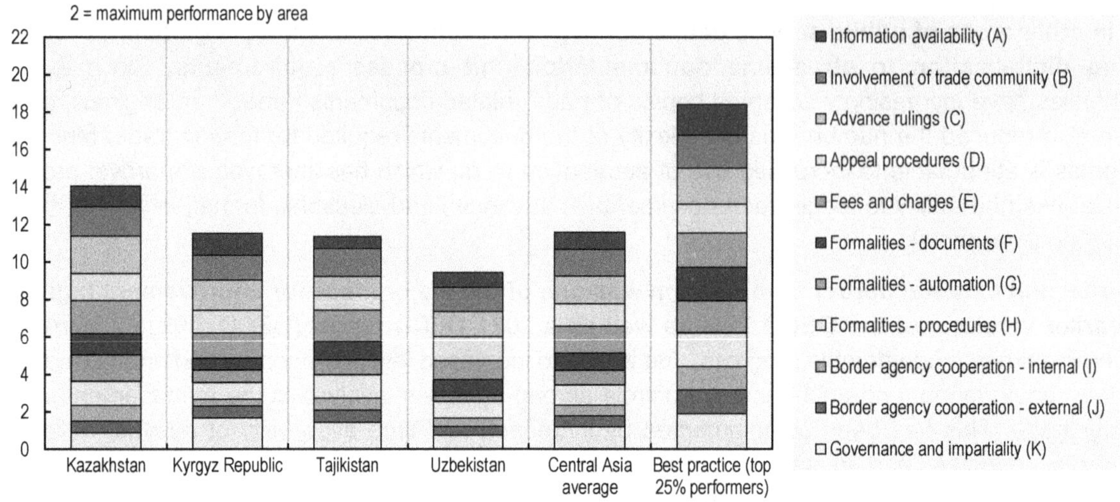

Source: (OECD, 2023[3])

Internal co-operation of government agencies in customs-related procedures is a challenge throughout Central Asia. Better data-sharing and coordination of customs-related interventions and policies could significantly improve the management of border and customs agencies, reducing the cost for trading firms. The government should enhance internal agency co-operation by improving internal co-ordination across public institutions, particularly those that conduct inspections of goods and issue certificates or permissions (OECD, 2021[1]). Developing interconnected transit information systems with other countries in the region and harmonising customs documents and requirements would also support external border agency co-operation.

5.3. Kazakhstan's private sector requires more reliable property rights protection and effective dispute resolution

A clear majority (55%) of survey respondents considered reforms to improve contract enforcement to be the number one reform priority for the government. Such reforms were also highlighted as one of the three priority areas for action by the OECD in 2021, with the Organisation placing an emphasis on the importance of the reliability of dispute settlement and contract enforcement, this reflecting firm-level feedback on the predictability of decisions relating to dispute resolution and property rights enforcement at that time (OECD, 2021[1]).

The government has made numerous efforts to improve the quality of contract enforcement. These efforts have been closely linked to the more transversal reform processes of reducing bureaucracy, addressing corruption and using digital technologies to improve efficiency and transparency in public service delivery. The progress in improving contract enforcement in many ways reflects reform progress in other policy areas. On the one hand, the legal and regulatory framework for contract enforcement and intellectual property protection is relatively strong, there are legal avenues for formal and alternative dispute resolution, and new institutions such as the Court of the Astana International Financial Centre (AIFC) have been established. On the other hand, respondent firms continue to raise concerns, particularly in terms of the predictability and impartiality of decisions.

The gap between the *de facto* experience of firms and the *de jure* provisions that ought protect them is a major point of concern. As with other policy areas that affect the private sector, the predictability of contract enforcement is a major determinant of a country's investment attractiveness (North, 1990[4]) (La Porta et al., 1997[5]). While new institutions such as the AIFC can be a welcome addition to the legal framework conditions for business, there is a risk that such special centres become islands within the legal landscape. That a foreign firm can be assured of highly competent common law judges may well raise the attractiveness of Kazakhstan as an investment destination, but that attractiveness will be decidedly lessened if an investor perceives the legal landscape in which their potential suppliers and clients operate lacks the predictability offered to them.

5.3.1. The legal framework for contract enforcement and dispute settlement

Kazakhstan has a clear and well-developed legal framework for contract enforcement and dispute settlement. The legal framework for contract disputes is clearly set out in Article 27 of the Civil Code (CC) which stipulates that both foreign investors and domestic businesses can seek dispute settlement either in Kazakhstan's courts or at international arbitration, with Kazakhstan's courts required by law to enforce contractual arbitration clauses (Art. 501, 502, 503 CC) (Republic of Kazakhstan, 2005[6]), as well as arbitration awards. Kazakhstan is a signatory to the 1958 New York Convention on the Recognition and Enforcement of Foreign Arbitral Awards.

Efforts in recent years have focused on the procedural efficiency of the court system, which has been significantly streamlined. The Astana City Court and the Supreme Court are the only courts in Kazakhstan that consider investment dispute cases, and the government has established a Specialised Judicial Board under the Supreme Court for disputes related to the performance of mutual obligations under investment contracts between large investors and government bodies (OECD, 2018[7]). The Board is composed of seven judges of the Supreme Court, specialised in investment-disputes, and it acts as a Court of first instance (International Tax and Investment Center, 2016[8]). In addition, the legality of a wide range of ADR mechanisms for disputes between two private parties has been codified in the Entrepreneurial Code and the Law on Mediation.

Predictable contract enforcement with public agencies is important for expanding the role of the private sector in public-private partnerships (PPPs) and procurement, areas that are critical for issues such as increasing the level of private and foreign investment in sustainable infrastructure. Unpredictable contract enforcement with public agencies is a key issue for the ability and willingness of firms to enter into public private partnerships and public procurement agreements with the government or other public bodies. The perception that the public entities are not upholding contractual commitments on account of pressures arising from domestic economic conditions may undermine business confidence and damage the government's reputation as a reliable partner, reducing Kazakhstan's attractiveness as an investment destination (OECD, 2021[1]).

Recent efforts under the Supreme Court's "Seven Pillar Strategy" have been targeting this issue, by focusing on the quality of court decisions to raise both the quality and coherence of judgements, and the trust of businesses and citizens in the judicial bodies. As a first step, the Supreme Court has developed a decision template to guide the process of drafting judgements and increase its reliability. In addition, the reform also targets the skills and capacity of judicial staff through the development of a new system of judicial recruitment and oversight under the High Judicial Council. The focus is set on the selection and retention of competent judges, and enhanced training on drafting judgements in accordance with international standards.

As noted above, corruption is a transversal issue for the business community, and it applies to the judiciary as elsewhere. Concerns about judicial corruption and integrity continue to undermine business confidence. Some of the major issues in this regard are: judicial staff lacking employment security due to an absence of tenured positions and low remuneration; political supervision of court judgements by chiefs of courts or public prosecutors; and lack of automated case management (OECD, 2017[9]). Such problems may dissuade foreign investors from entering Kazakhstan, and may discourage domestic firms from pursuing dispute resolution through formal avenues.

The protection of intellectual property (IP) rights is an essential element of a good business climate and can play a key role in helping to attract investors with proprietary technologies. The legal framework for IP rights in Kazakhstan has improved greatly over time, notably through harmonisation of international best practices as part of Kazakhstan's accession to the WTO and ratification of World Intellectual Property Organisation (WIPO) treaties.

Despite extensive legal provisions for guaranteeing IPR (the Civil Code, the Law on Patents, and the Law on Copyrights and Neighbouring Rights), enforcement proceeds through civil and criminal courts where judges lack specialised IPR knowledge. No designated public institution seems to be responsible for managing IPR disputes, nor is there evidence that public organisations that do have a role in IPR-related disputes have clearly defined responsibilities and functions.

5.3.2. Broadening the use of alternative dispute resolution

Kazakhstan has begun to develop a comprehensive legal framework for alternative dispute resolution (ADR), bringing the country closer to international best practices and legal standards. The Law on Arbitration, which governs dispute settlement for both domestic and international businesses, has brought national legislation in line with the United Nations Commission on International Trade Law (UNCITRAL) Model on International Commercial Arbitration, the New York Convention on the Recognition and Enforcement of Foreign Arbitral Awards, and the European Convention on International Commercial Arbitration. However, investors cite a number of shortcomings in the legal regulation for initiating and managing arbitration procedures, particularly as regards the impartiality of the necessary institutions and the transparency in their relations to the parties, be they public or private (OECD, 2021[1]). Since 2017, the Supreme Court has given priority to the development of ADR and mediation under the seven-pillar strategy, launching pilot court annexed and out-of-court mediation programmes in early 2019, complemented by outreach activities to increase the awareness of citizens on mediation (OECD, n.d.[10]).

The framework nevertheless requires further development, and there remain issues around the impartiality of ADR processes, particularly in public-private disputes. For the resolution of disputes between government organisations and local companies, government organisations need to obtain the consent of the relevant ministry. Given the high share of SOEs among medium and large enterprises, this requirement hinders arbitration processes (NCE "Atameken", 2019[11]). In the last Investment Policy Review of Kazakhstan, launched in 2017, the OECD noted that mediation, though foreseen in the legislation as a valid means of dispute resolution, was not at that point widely used (OECD, n.d.[10]). For investors to have clarity and certainty, it is imperative that the right to initiate arbitration proceedings is codified in the contract *ex ante* and not introduced when parties are already in dispute. At the same time, as in other CIS countries, the ability of the Supreme Court to overturn arbitration rulings on the pretext of malpractice "oversight" undermines the legal certainty of the process, reducing its appeal to international and domestic firms.

The government has created a business ombudsman, the Commissioner for Protection of the Rights of Entrepreneurs of Kazakhstan under the National Chamber of Entrepreneurs. This institution could play an important role in out-of-court dispute settlement (OECD, 2018[12]). It receives complaints from businesses about unfair treatment by government authorities, including instances of maladministration and unfair law enforcement, such as repetitive audits or inspections, unreasonable fines and penalties, or threats and acts of retaliation by officials. The Commissioner also sends recommendations to state bodies and can recommend prosecution of the relevant state authority. From 2016 to 2018, the Ombudsman received 17,053 appeals, 46% of which received full or partial outcomes (OECD, 2021[1]). The decreasing trend in the number of appeals is attributed to a positive dynamic of lower number of complaints submitted to the Ombudsman each year (NCE "Atameken", 2019[11]). However, it could also be attributable to a diminishing impact and of an initial backlog of complaints. Disputes are concentrated in such areas as land, tax, law enforcement, and public procurement, the rest being mainly related to administrative barriers, investments or loans (Ombudsman for the Protection of the Rights of Entrepreneurs of Kazakhstan, 2019[13]). Sixty percent of respondents to the survey assessed the creation of the Business Ombudsman as useful or very useful for foreign investors; however, 37% could not give an evaluation of such a measure.

However, general rule of law concerns remain, particularly regarding enforcement of international arbitration rulings in domestic courts (EBRD, 2015[14]; World Justice Project, 2019[15]; OECD, n.d.[10]). Despite a legal requirement to do so, enforcement problems have been known to arise. To support dispute resolution, the government has expanded ADR services. In what was a first in Central Asia, it established the Astana International Financial Centre to support international arbitration through an English-law governed International Arbitration Centre (IAC) for civil and commercial disputes. When asked about the effective measures implemented to assist foreign investors, 70% of respondents to the survey considered that the establishment of the AIFC was either useful or very useful. However, the IAC has so far been used too rarely to assess its effectiveness in handling disputes, having handled 1743 arbitration and mediation cases since its establishment in 2018 (IAC, 2023[16]). In addition, for the IAC to contribute to the creation of a wider arbitration culture in Kazakhstan, the government should ensure that best practices are shared with domestic courts and that investors and businesses routinely have sufficient certainty that local jurisdictions will enforce IAC awards.

References

Council of Europe (2019), *Action Document for EU-Central Asia Rule of Law Programme*, https://rm.coe.int/ca-project-one-page-summary/16809fb95a. [23]

EBRD (2015), *Business Environment and Enterprise Performance Survey (BEEPS) V: Kazakhstan*, https://beeps-ebrd.com/wp-content/uploads/2015/09/kazakhstan.pdf. [14]

IAC (2023), *International Arbitration Centre*, AIFC, Astan, https://iac.aifc.kz/en. [16]

International Tax and Investment Center (2016), *Kazakh Supreme Court Specialized Board on Investor Disputes*, https://www.iticnet.org/blog/2016/01/07/kazakh-supreme-court-specialized-board-on-investor-disputes. [8]

ITF (2019), "Enhancing Connectivity and Freight in Central Asia", *International Transport Forum Policy Papers*, No. 71, OECD Publishing, Paris, https://doi.org/10.1787/0492621a-en. [2]

La Porta, R. et al. (1997), *Legal Determinants of External Finance*, https://doi.org/10.1111/j.1540-6261.1997.tb02727.x. [5]

NCE "Atameken" (2019), *National Report on Entrepreneurship in Kazakhstan*. [11]

North, D. (1990), *Institutions, Institutional Change, and Economic Performance*, Cambridge University Press, https://doi.org/10.1017/CBO9780511808678. [4]

OECD (2023), *OECD Trade Facilitation Indicators*, Uzbekistan, OECD Publishing, Paris, https://www.oecd.org/trade/topics/trade-facilitation/. [3]

OECD (2021), *Improving the Legal Environment for Business and Investment in Central Asia*, OECD Publishing, Paris, https://www.oecd.org/eurasia/Improving-LEB-CA-ENG%2020%20April.pdf. [1]

OECD (2021), *Improving the Legal Environment for Business and Investment in Central Asia*, OECD Publishing, Paris, https://www.oecd.org/eurasia/Improving-LEB-CA-ENG%2020%20April.pdf. [17]

OECD (2021), *Informality and COVID-19 in Eurasia: The Sudden Loss of a Social Buffer*, OECD Eurasia Policy Insights, OECD Publishing, Paris, https://www.oecd.org/eurasia/COVID-19-informality-Eurasia.pdf. [18]

OECD (2021), *OECD Skills Strategy Kazakhstan*, OECD Skills Studies, OECD Publishing, Paris, https://www.oecd-ilibrary.org/docserver/39629b47-en.pdf?expires=1680001847&id=id&accname=ocid84004878&checksum=D3595A6C0999F042419701A870241E13. [20]

OECD (2020), *OECD investment policy responses to COVID-19.* [25]

OECD (2019), *OECD Trade Facilitation Indicators*, http://www.oecd.org/trade/topics/trade-facilitation/. [26]

OECD (2018), *Reforming Kazakhstan: Progress, Challenges and Opportunities.* [7]

OECD (2018), *SME and Entrepreneurship Policy in Kazakhstan.* [12]

OECD (2017), *4th round of monitoring of the Istanbul Anti-Corruption Action Plan: Kazakhstan.* [9]

OECD (2017), *Anti-Corruption Reforms in Kazakhstan: 4th Round of Monitoring of the Istanbul Anti-Corruption Action Plan*, OECD Publishing, Paris, https://www.oecd.org/corruption/acn/OECD-ACN-Kazakhstan-Round-4-Monitoring-Report-ENG.pdf. [19]

OECD (n.d.), *OECD Investment Policy Reviews*, OECD Publishing, Paris, https://doi.org/10.1787/19900910. [10]

OECD (n.d.), *OECD Policy Responses to Coronavirus (COVID-19)*, OECD Publishing, Paris, https://doi.org/10.1787/5b0fd8cd-en. [29]

OECD (n.d.), *OECD Policy Responses to Coronavirus (COVID-19)*, OECD Publishing, Paris, https://doi.org/10.1787/5b0fd8cd-en. [30]

Ombudsman for the Protection of the Rights of Entrepreneurs of Kazakhstan (2019), *Annual Report*, https://ombudsmanbiz.kz/details/ndownload.php?fn=31&lang=rus. [13]

Republic of Kazakhstan (2015), *Law on the High Judicial Council (No. 436-IV)*, https://www.venice.coe.int/webforms/documents/default.aspx?pdffile=CDL-REF(2018)050-e. [22]

Republic of Kazakhstan (2005), *Civil Code of Kazakhstan*, http://adilet.zan.kz/eng/docs/K940001000_. [6]

Transparency International (2018), *Customs corruption in Kazakhstan: a trade mirror analysis*, https://knowledgehub.transparency.org/product/customs-corruption-in-kazakhstan-a-trade-mirror-analysis. [27]

US Department of State (2019), *2019 Investment Climate: Kazakhstan*, https://www.state.gov/reports/2019-investment-climate-statements/kazakhstan/. [24]

World Bank (2019), *World Bank Indicators*, https://data.worldbank.org/indicator. [21]

World Justice Project (2019), *WJP Rule of Law Index*, https://www.worldjusticeproject.org/rule-of-law-index/ (accessed on 8 July 2020). [15]

WTO (2023), *Notification Requirements: Trade Facilitation Agreement*, WTO, Geneva, https://notifications.wto.org/en/notification-requirements/trade-facilitation-agreement. [28]

Notes

[1] As elsewhere in this report, percentages relating to the survey include the 27 firm respondents and four organisational respondents (e.g., trade representation offices or business associations).

[2] As part of the accession process to the World Trade Organisation (WTO), a country is required to make certain commitments in various areas to ensure compliance with WTO rules and regulations. These commitments are split across three categories (A, B and C). Commitments in Category A refer to the implementation of WTO provisions as soon as a country becomes a member; commitments in Category B refer to transitional periods that a country may require for implementing certain WTO provisions, allowing the acceding country time to make adjustments to domestic laws and regulations to ensure compliance; commitments in Category C relate to technical assistance and capacity-building measures, acknowledging that some acceding countries may require additional support and resources to implement WTO agreements (WTO, 2023[28]).

6 Facilitating and encouraging foreign investment: Focus on regulatory barriers and competition

Respondents to the survey were largely committed to retaining or interested in potentially expanding their activities in Kazakhstan in spite of international political and economic turbulence. While positive assessment of survey respondents is welcome, the actual ability of the government to attract and retain foreign investment continues to be mitigated by regulatory barriers and competition issues.

6.1. Survey observations and overview

Policies to support foreign investors were among those assessed most positively by survey respondents. Flagship projects such as the establishment of the Astana International Financial Centre and the creation of special economic zones were among the top three policies rated as very useful by respondents (Figure 6.1). A plurality of respondents also rated a range of other policies and reforms – from the creation of the Foreign Investors' Council to investment promotion and facilitation services – as either very or somewhat useful. It is encouraging for the government, as it proceeds with its investment agenda, that policy interventions that have been explicitly designed to facilitate the entry and operation of foreign investors are being received positively by the business community.

On each of the indicators, only a small number of respondents reported that they were not useful. The survey results suggest that policy interventions have on the whole been generally well designed and targeted, easing to varying degrees the entry and operation of foreign firms in the country. In certain cases, respondents may not have benefited directly from policies captured by the indicator – for example, special economic zones or investment promotion services – but that they are nevertheless positively assessed indicates an awareness and appreciation within the business community of the positive impact of a broad array of policy interventions.

The policies captured in the survey reflect a concerted effort by the government to make it easier for foreign firms to do business in Kazakhstan. Creating an investor-friendly regulatory framework that allows foreign firms to contribute to the development of the local private sector and the economy more broadly has been a key ambition of the government for decades. In 2022, this ambition was reiterated through the new Investment Policy Concept of the Republic of Kazakhstan until 2026, which outlined a headline target of increasing the inflow of FDI to USD 25.5 billion by 2026 (the "Concept") (Kazakh Invest, 2022[1]). At the core of the Concept was recognition of the need to increase investment in non-resource sectors of the economy. At first glance, the government's policy framework appears to be speaking to the needs of the types of firms the country wants to target.

Figure 6.1. Firm-level evaluation of the status of reforms in Kazakhstan

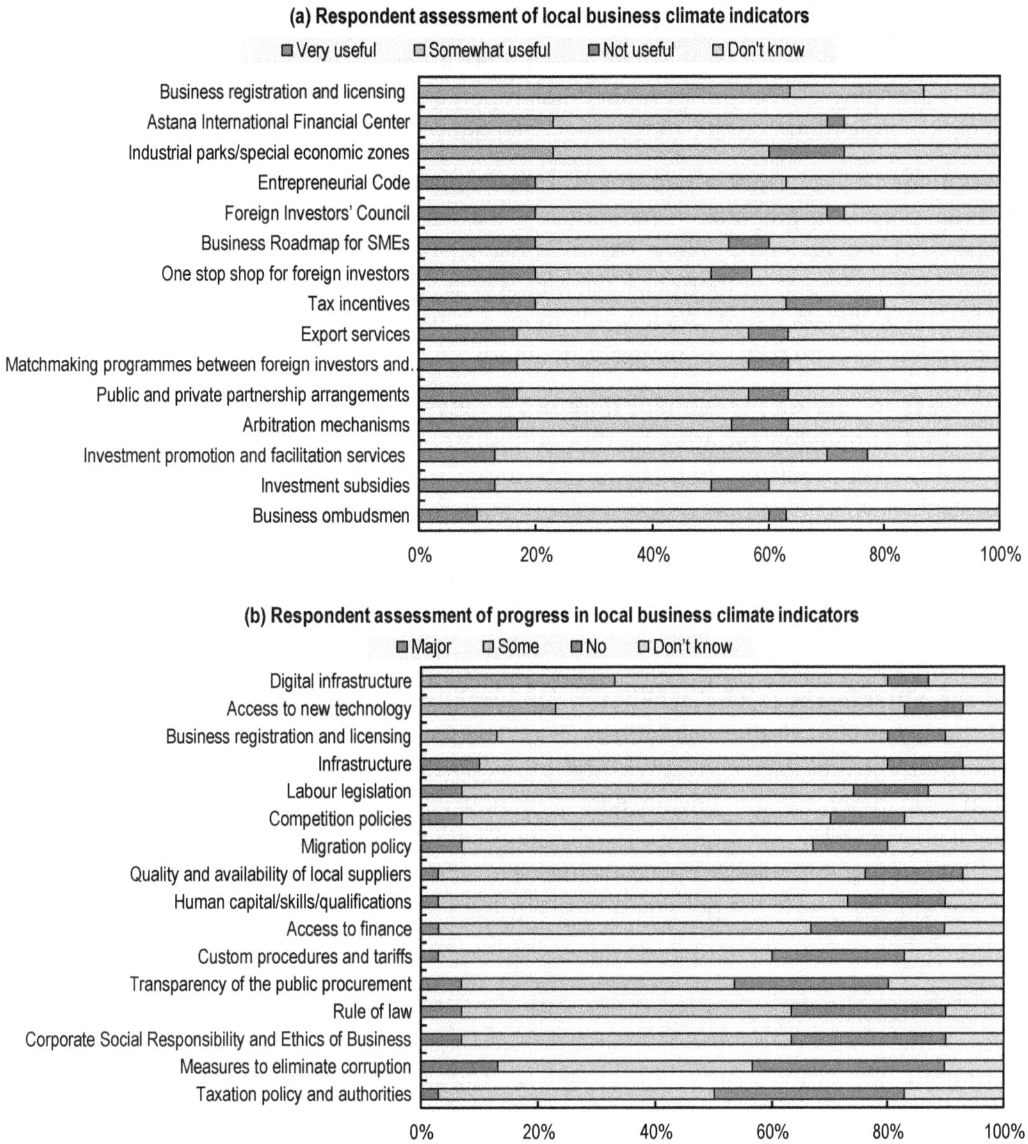

Note: As a percentage of the total number of respondents.
Source: EU-OECD Business Climate Assessment Survey in Kazakhstan

Nevertheless, two issues arise that could give cause for concern for the government. The first relates to the relative lack of progress in the broader de jure and de facto environment for business, as indicated in (Figure 6.1 b). Of 16 business-climate indicators included in the survey, 15% or more of respondents noted major progress in only four: digital infrastructure, access to new technology, business registration and licensing, and measures to eliminate corruption. It is equally clear that respondents see some kind of progress in each of these areas, but the extent to which this progress has significantly changed the perception of firms on a number of major considerations for doing business in Kazakhstan – for example, competition – appears to be limited.

The second point is that the impact of reforms to support foreign investors on actual investment flows will be limited if they are not accompanied by complementary pro-competition and pro-market reforms. A sub-indicator on competition policies highlights the importance of ensuring that simpler reforms, such as the simplification of licensing and permitting, are accompanied by pro-competition efforts. Respondents generally accept that the institutional framework for competition is adequate, but they are significantly less positive about individual aspects of competition policy and its implementation. Some 62% of respondents, for example, claim that the government's control of market dominance and monopoly practices in the economy is weak, while around half report that the government's efforts to combat cartels and market concentration (48% and 52% respectively) are poor.

Survey responses indicate that a two-speed reform process may be emerging. On the one hand, there has been significant progress in modernising the framework conditions necessary for the future competitiveness of the economy: more digital services, better access to technologies, better digital infrastructure. At the same time, there has been slower progress in addressing underlying and at times transversal business climate issues. As a result, there is a risk that laudable government efforts in certain areas will be undermined by a lack of progress in others.

The impediments to foreign investment may not be investment regulation itself, but the adjacent policy areas that shape the broader business climate. Kazakhstan has a relatively open statutory framework for FDI, but regulatory barriers to investment remain. Investment and trade in services, for example, is still highly regulated, while key network sectors of the economy remain under state control. This means that while a firm may face relatively few restrictions in entering a given sector, it may face a range of regulatory and competition-related issues once it enters the market. Many of these issues may in the first instance affect local firms, but they also make the practicalities of doing business in Kazakhstan more difficult for foreign firms.

Increasing the attractiveness of Kazakhstan for foreign investors is particularly important in the context of the green and digital transitions. Kazakhstan requires significant investment into many of the most restricted sectors of the economy – energy, electricity production, transport, telecommunications, infrastructure – in order for the private sector to navigate and benefit from the twin transitions of environmental sustainability and digitalisation. Rationalising the remaining barriers to investment in these sectors and addressing the adjacent policy issues that affect the general attractiveness of the business climate are therefore critical to the government's long-term development ambitions.

6.2. Kazakhstan has developed a strong *de jure* framework for investment

The government has significantly liberalised its regulatory framework for foreign investment. Kazakhstan has removed a significant number of investment-related restrictions, and the majority of the economy is, *de jure*, open to FDI. Kazakhstan scores slightly better than the non-OECD average on the OECD FDI Regulatory Restrictiveness Index, though it is still almost twice as restrictive as the OECD average.

The government has developed a broadly sound legal framework for investment and has implemented series of reforms to foster investment and entrepreneurial activities. In the *2018-2022 National Investment Strategy*, the government set out measures to improve the investment climate, privatisation plans and broader economic investment policy, with the aim of increasing total FDI inflows by 25% by 2022 (OECD, 2021[2]). In 2022, the government yet again updated its strategic policy aims for the investment climate through the *Investment Policy Concept of the Republic of Kazakhstan until 2026*, which replaced the percentage increase target of FDI inflows with a fixed sum of USD 25.5 billion by 2026.

A number of institutions and platforms have been created in recent years to ease the entry of foreign investors and to manage concerns that they raise more efficiently. In 2019, the government created the *Co-ordination Council for Attracting Foreign Investment*, of which the Prime Minister is the chair, with the council acting as an ombudsman for the investment community. The Investment Committee under the Ministry of Foreign Affairs and the investment promotion body Kazakh Invest, which operates under its aegis, manage investment policy issues and interface with potential and current investors; Kazakh Invest's *Investor Service Centres* were considered very useful by 13% of respondents and somewhat useful by 57%. Relations with international organisations and global bodies such as the WTO are generally managed by the Ministry of National Economy and the Ministry of Trade and Integration. The Astana International Financial Center (AIFC) was established in 2018 with a aim of creating a major regional financial hub in Kazakhstan that could serve the broader Central Asia region.

Investment activity is regulated by the Entrepreneurial Code (the "EC"), introduced in 2016, which superseded the 2003 Law on Investments and a range of other business-related legislation. The EC provides businesses and investors with more detailed guarantees on protection of rights and property, particularly against expropriation and unlawful official conduct. It provides for increased consistency and transparency of the applicable rules, for the protection of different categories of investment, and for stability of contracts between investors and the state (OECD, 2021[2]).

Kazakhstan has also made it a legal requirement to put forward any proposed new laws or amendments for public consultation. The EC is supplemented by the Law on Legal Acts (Subsection 8 Para. 4. Art. 18), which stipulates that any legal amendments or drafts must be put forward for public discussion on an online portal before being submitted to the relevant government institutions for consideration and agreement (Republic of Kazakhstan, 2019[3]). The Foreign Investor Council (FIC), which operates as a high-level public-private dialogue platform, was established by the government to allow investor concerns to be quickly identified and addressed; the work of the FIC was considered very useful by 20% of respondents and somewhat useful by a further 50%.

Nevertheless, the extent to which information on legal requirements is readily available to firms and the extent to which public institutions are transparent in their business-related decision-making remain unclear. For instance, the FIC, the main consultation body for foreign investors, does not publicise the summaries and official documents of its working groups. In addition, information relating to sectoral restrictions for international investors is not freely available, and a lack of English-language information, despite the recent creation of an online portal, may act as an informal barrier for foreign investors.

6.2.1. Kazakhstan scores well in the OECD FDI Regulatory Restrictiveness Index

The OECD FDI Regulatory Restrictiveness Index measures statutory restrictions on foreign investment in a range of sectors. Statutory restrictions can cover a number of areas and generally determine the extent to which there are discriminatory measures that affect foreign investors, both in terms of market access and national treatment. These can include equity restrictions, investment screening, restrictions on hiring personnel, and operational restrictions (e.g., land ownership, capital repatriation, etc.). The index is not a systematic assessment of the investment climate, and there are a number of policy settings that may affect FDI attractiveness that are not captured by the indicator. Kazakhstan performs fairly well in the indicator, relative to both the OECD and non-OECD averages, and it is the second most open economy in Central Asia from a statutory point of view.

The OECD has found that countries with a relatively open regulatory regime tend to receive higher FDI inflows relative to GDP (Mistura and Roulet, 2019[4]). Yet, as demonstrated by Kazakhstan's relatively strong performance in the indicator (Figure 6.2), regulatory openness to investment does not guarantee that investment will be forthcoming. Flows are affected by a wide range of other factors, including policy settings and the business climate, but also location, resource endowments, market access and market size.

Figure 6.2. OECD FDI Regulatory Restrictiveness Index: Kazakhstan (2020)

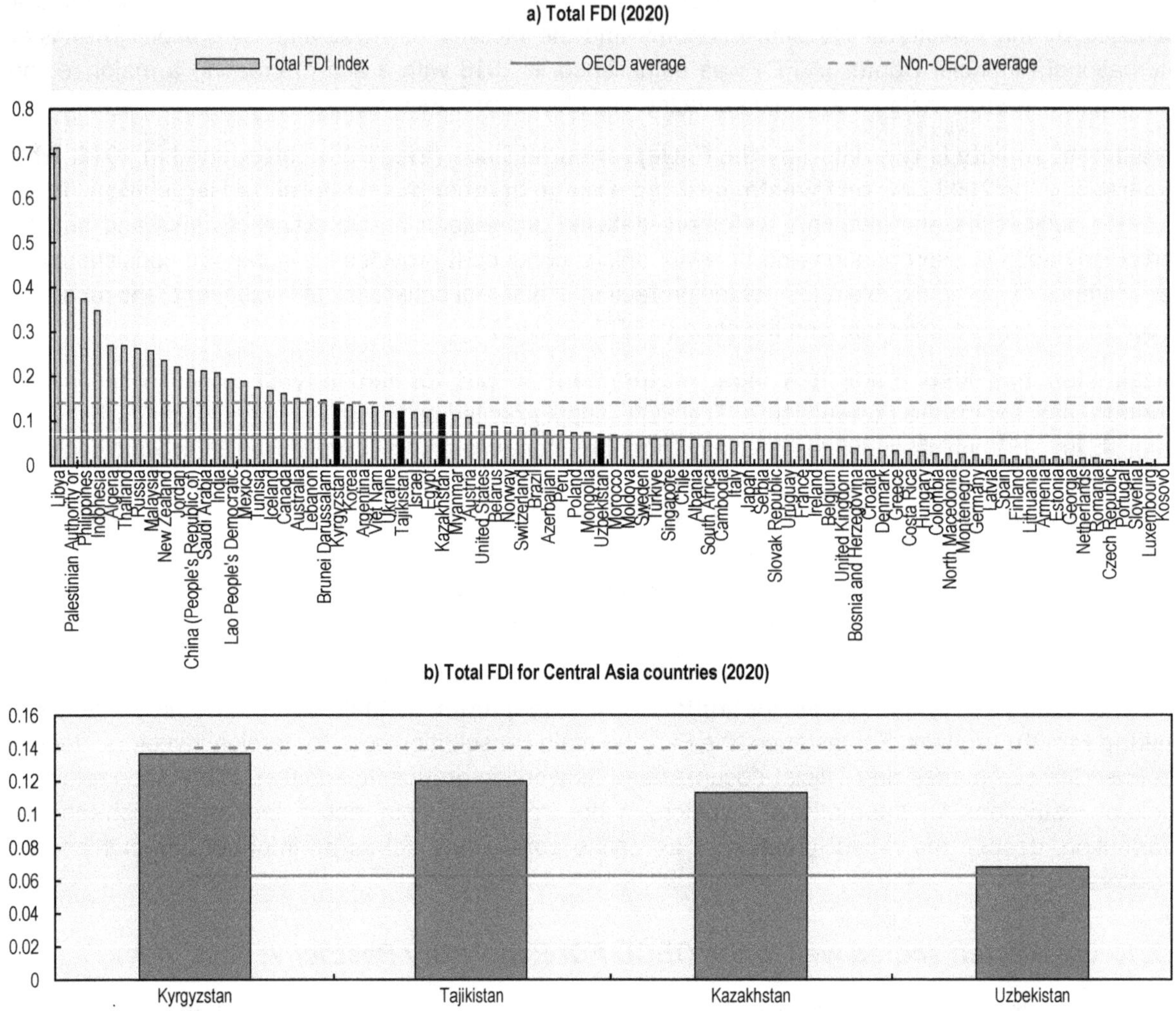

Source: (OECD, 2023[5])

Some sectors nevertheless remain restricted, notably service sectors such as media, air transport, banking and insurance, and fixed telecommunications, although existing equity restrictions in air transport and fixed telecoms were removed in early 2016, partly as part of WTO accession (Fig. 6.2) (OECD, 2021[2]). The restrictions in these sectors also correspond to observations on state-ownership and control and restrictions on services trade in other OECD analyses, as discussed below. Foreign investors in resource sectors also face restrictions relating to the use of agricultural and forested land. While foreign land users are not entitled to own land, private ownership of land plots is permitted if related to business activities. Further reforms continue to take place in connection with WTO accession, including the 2020 reform that allowed foreign banks and insurance companies to establish branches in Kazakhstan (OECD, 2022[6]). Once these reforms are accomplished, Kazakhstan will be close to the OECD average in terms of restrictiveness. Foreign participation in privatisation is not restricted.

Figure 6.3. OECD FDI Regulatory Restrictiveness Index, sectoral level: Kazakhstan (2020)

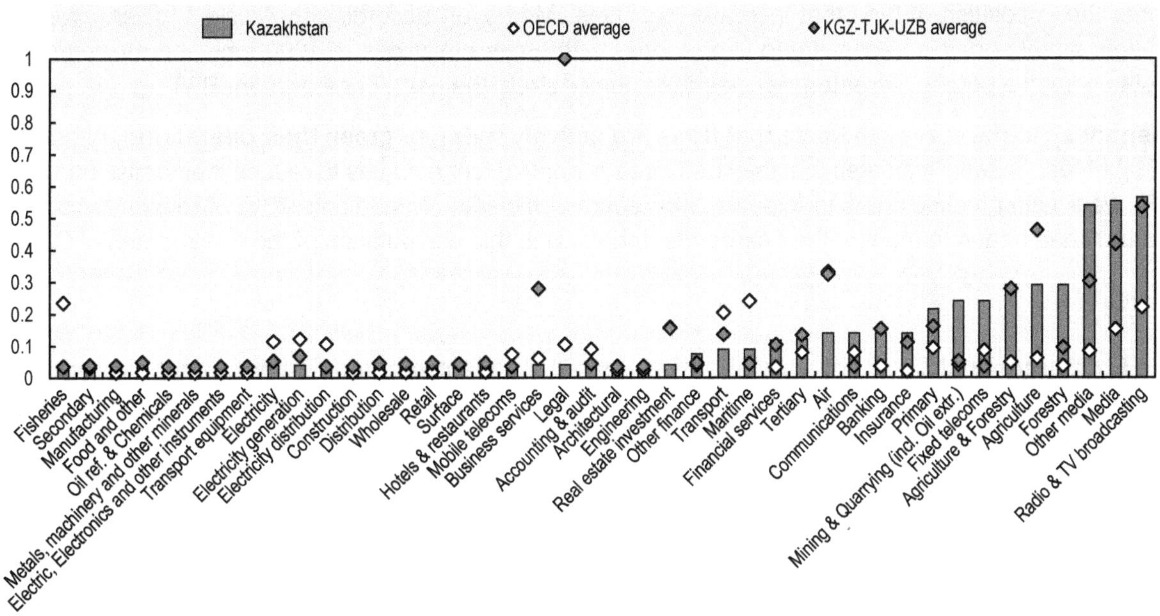

Source: (OECD, 2023[5])

Businesses still face burdensome conditions with regard to the employment of key foreign personnel, although this is also becoming simpler as a result of WTO accession. Kazakhstan's visa policy has been seen by investors as presenting an unnecessary obstacle to investment, as specific conditions include labour market tests for foreign managers and specialists hired in Kazakhstan in the framework of intra-corporate transfer; limitations on the number of foreigners for each category of corporate employees; regulatory quotas for work permits; and preferential treatment of domestic suppliers in the subsoil sector (OECD, 2018[7]).

6.2.2. The government has addressed certain long-standing regulatory concerns, but regulatory issues nevertheless remain

This section introduces a selected number of regulatory problems that have a broad significance for the private sector in the context of diversification and decarbonisation. It draws attention to a number of improvements and challenges in the regulatory landscape for investors that are adjacent to investment policy.

The new Environmental Code provides greater clarity about firms' environmental responsibilities

The government introduced a new Environmental Code in January 2021, which aimed to regulate activities of any individual of legal entity that could potentially have a negative impact on the environment, such as carbon emissions or other forms of pollution. The Environmental Code also supports the introduction of the best available techniques (BAT) in the country, bringing Kazakhstan's regulatory framework for environmental management closer to OECD best practices. In the context of the ongoing push for decarbonisation, the Environmental Code provides needed clarity for firms in the oil and gas, mining and metallurgical, chemical and electric power industries, which are responsible for a large share of pollution in the country (IEA, 2022[8]).

The implementation of BAT mostly relies on a mix of financial and non-financial incentives. Under Article 127, fees can now be charged for emissions of pollutants into the air; non-compliance with BAT will trigger the imposition of fees that increase over time. Moreover, according to Article 111, an *integrated environmental permit* is necessary to use facilities with gross emissions of 1000 tons and more. In order to obtain such a permit, the enterprise needs to demonstrate the use of one or more BAT.

Responses to the survey indicate that firms are actively trying to green their operations. Almost half (48%) of respondents indicated that they had already applied technologies to reduce their emissions, while 42% were using technologies to improve their energy efficiency. In addition, 26% of respondents noted that they had begun to monitor their carbon footprints, with this a stipulation of the Environmental Code.

Uncertainty on legal issues relating to expropriation remain

The Entrepreneurial Code protects all investors are legally protected against direct expropriation ("nationalisation and requisition"). Art. 276 stipulates that investors can obtain damages as compensation for illegal government action or inaction. Assets can only be seized in exceptional cases, justified on specific grounds (mainly linked to national security) and with due compensation paid in full. Also, though the EC allows the state to nationalise or requisition property only in specified cases, it does not clearly define such cases, nor does it define the method for calculating compensation.

The law is less clear about cases of indirect expropriation where the investor still holds the property title but where government measures have an impact on the property that is considered tantamount to expropriation. The lack of clear statutory protections against indirect expropriation may lead to cases where regulatory changes create grounds for license or permit revocations, denying businesses recourse to compensation (OECD, n.d.[9]). In the case of environmental licensing, businesses have reported cases where violations arising from unexpected regulatory changes have been used as leverage in negotiations with the government (OECD, n.d.[9]).

Kazakhstan is a signatory to several international investment agreements (IIAs) which protect covered investors against expropriation without compensation and discrimination, and grant access to investor-state dispute settlement mechanisms (ISDS). Under Kazakh IIAs, the state may not expropriate except for public interest purposes, on a non-discriminatory basis, under due process of law and with prompt, adequate and effective compensation (the so-called Hull formula). Unlike the EC, Kazakh IIAs do explicitly cover indirect expropriation, although they do not clarify which regulatory changes would not amount to expropriation, such as for public safety, health and the environment. This ambiguity could leave Kazakhstan vulnerable to challenges by investors in the event that regulatory changes affect the profitability or viability of their operations.

Land ownership continues to be a regulatory challenge for certain foreign investors

Land in Kazakhstan is owned by the state but can be transferred, sold or leased to individuals or legal entities. Most leases are for 49 years, down from 99 years in early legislation. The Land Code adopted on 20 June 2003 (last amended in 2019) establishes the foundations, conditions and limits for modifying or terminating ownership of land and land-use rights, and describes the rights and responsibilities of landowners and land-users and regulates land relations. Land reform in Kazakhstan, as in some other parts of the former Soviet Union, has been a slow and at times difficult process, particularly concerning agricultural land.

Foreign nationals and legal entities (defined as those with majority foreign control) are allowed to own land for business related purposes (production or non-production facilities and land to service such facilities), but foreign ownership of agricultural and forest land is not, permitted. In order to reduce the share of unused land and enhance the better use of cultivated agricultural land, the government amended the 2003 Land Code in 2015 to allow foreign tenancy of land for up to 25 years (from 10 years previously) and the purchase of land for agricultural purposes by private residents. However, in 2016, the government adopted a five-year moratorium on application of the amendments due to public dissatisfaction with them; in 2021, this moratorium was then extended by another five years. Since 2018, work has been underway to revise the amendments and develop mechanisms to achieve their original aim, that is, to eliminate barriers to more effective agricultural land use.

In 2021, a new, much stricter law on land ownership was adopted. I provided for a total ban on the transfer and sale of agricultural land to foreign individuals and companies. The new legislation has nevertheless been accompanied with other measures that may improve transparency around land ownership in the country, with the government due to open the information stored on the state land cadastre to the public (Ageleuov, 2021[10]).

The right of the state to expropriate land applies only in circumstances set out in the Land Code. For instance, the state may expropriate land if it is being used contrary to its legal designation or in violation of the law, or where the state has an exceptional need for the land and where a compromise has been made between the state and the land user. Conflicts concerning land confiscation arise at the *akimat* level. The Land Code assumes that compensation can be either monetary or in-kind (equivalent land). In practice, *akimats* do not always offer equivalent land (OECD, 2021[2]).

6.3. Kazakhstan retains a number of regulatory barriers to services trade

While the overall regulatory framework for investment in Kazakhstan is relatively open, there are a number of restrictions on potential FDI that relate to services sectors. Many of restrictions that remain are in crucial service sectors necessary for the broader competitiveness of the economy. Obstacles to services trade are pervasive in many OECD and non-OECD economies, often due to the somewhat siloed nature of service-sector regulators, which can limit the ability to foresee or consider the impact of a regulation on other areas of the economy or the economy more broadly.

The OECD Services Trade Restrictiveness Index (STRI) provides additional insights into regulatory restrictions on trade and investment that may not be captured by the OECD FDI Regulatory Restrictiveness Index. The results of the STRI point to some of the challenges faced by investors in Kazakhstan, as well as testifying to the progress that the country has made liberalising the investment regime since WTO accession in 2015.

Overall, Kazakhstan can be seen to be more restrictive than the OECD average, and it is among the most restrictive of the 50 economies covered by the index (Figure 6.4). This score reflects, *inter alia*, work permitting issues for foreign nationals looking to provide short-term services, the maintenance of foreign investment screening mechanisms, limited access to public procurement for foreign service suppliers (albeit there are time-bound exceptions to this arrangement), and the above-mentioned restrictions on the acquisition of land and real estate by foreigners.

Figure 6.4. OECD Services Trade Restrictiveness Index (2022)

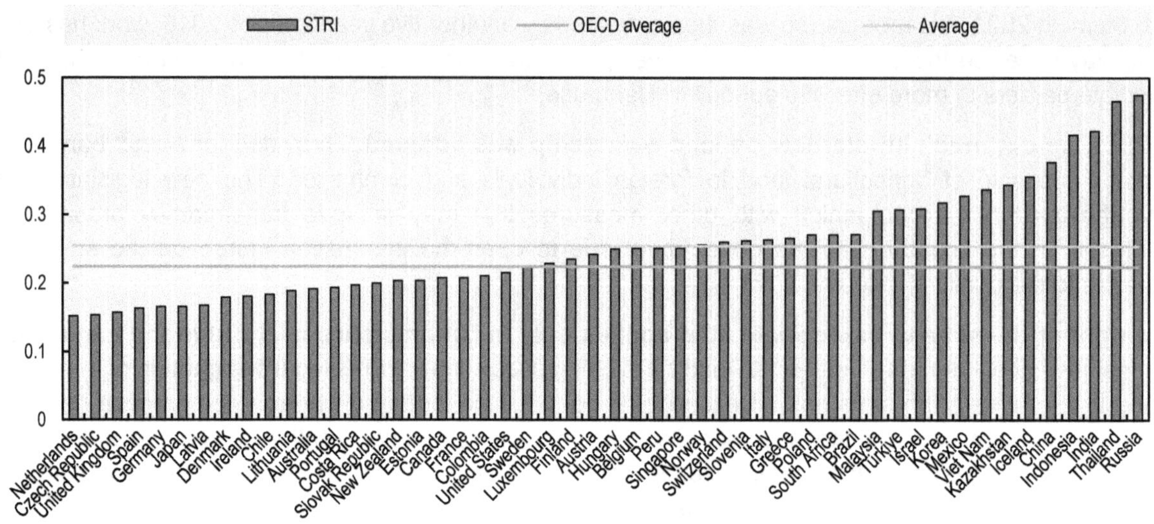

Source: (OECD, 2022[6])

Services trade restrictions have nevertheless been relaxed in recent years, likely in part due to the country's WTO accession commitments. The highest levels of liberalisation can be seen in courier services (Figure 6.5), with the postal services sector now more open to competition following a reform in 2017 that abolished the natural monopoly regulation of the postal service. There has also been liberalisation in the insurance services sector, thanks to a 2018 decision that abolished a rule that required reinsurance companies to be incorporated in Kazakhstan. There has been liberalisation in many other service sectors, though of a smaller magnitude.

Figure 6.5. OECD Services Trade Restrictiveness Index: Kazakhstan (2014-2022)

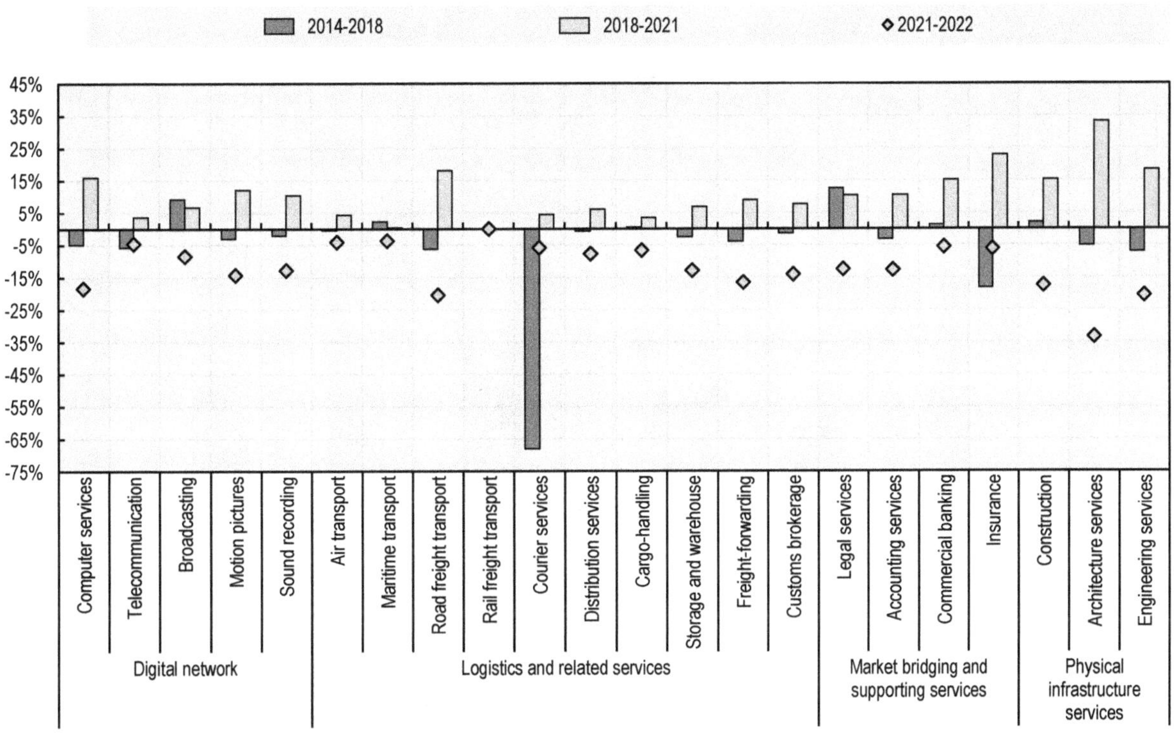

Source: (OECD, 2022[6])

The most heavily regulated service sectors in Kazakhstan are related to a number of areas where policy action could significantly improve the business climate for both domestic and international firms. For example, rail freight transport continues to be highly regulated, with the state having a total monopoly in this area. Significant barriers also exist in telecommunications and banking services (Figure 6.6), two areas where Kazakhstan requires significant investment if the private sector is to equip itself for the digital and green transitions.

Figure 6.6. OECD Services Trade Restrictiveness Index: Kazakhstan and the world average (2022)

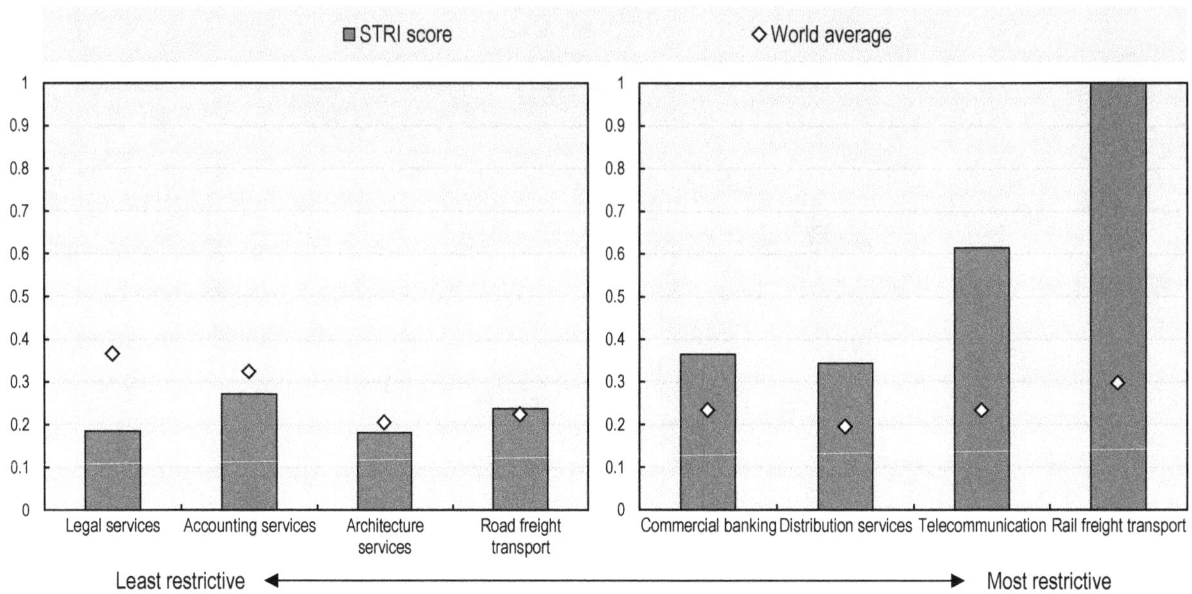

Source: (OECD, 2022[6])

Levels of investment in telecommunications and the general quality of connectivity services are low, which may in part be attributable to a lack of competition in the sector. Kazakhstan has the fourth-most restricted telecommunications sector in the economies covered by the STRI database. Liberalisation of the telecommunications sector could help reduce barriers to investment in the digital and connectivity infrastructure necessary for the private sector to make the most of the digital transition.

Figure 6.7. OECD Services Trade Restrictiveness Index: Telecommunications (2022)

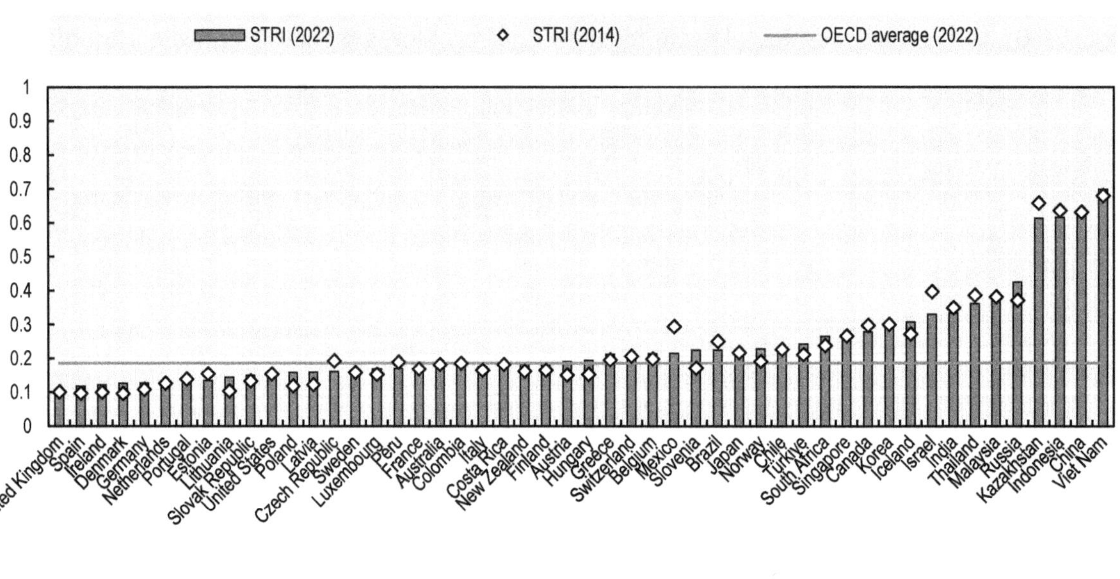

Source: (OECD, 2022[6])

6.4. Competition issues may undermine investment promotion

The OECD Indicators of Product Market Regulation (PMR) are another tool used by the OECD to assess the openness of an economy to investment. The PMR indicators focus more on competition. Kazakhstan is the only country in Central Asia included in the system of PMR indicators, with the last update being released in 2018. Taken together with Kazakhstan's relatively open regulatory regime for FDI, the PMRs give an opportunity to begin to identify a number of transversal policy and regulatory issues – such as the role of the state in key network sectors, the governance of SOEs, and distortions due to state involvement that may affect product markets – that might affect the investment attractiveness of the country.

Economy-wide regulatory conditions are less conducive to competition than the OECD average, though the country does perform similarly – in some cases better than – other emerging market economies. Nevertheless, the high-level results mask significant differences in the underlying regulatory areas. Distortions that are induced by the involvement of the state in a number of business sectors are significant, considerably more so than in most OECD countries, while the country continues to have entry barriers for both domestic and international competitors that are higher than the OECD average, if lower than most emerging market economies.

The most significant issue highlighted by the PMRs, and which again speaks to issues raised by the survey, is the extent of public ownership in the economy and the level of direct public control over enterprises. This, together with weak governance of state-owned enterprises (SOEs), creates significant imbalances in the playing field that not only affects the attractiveness of the country for foreign investors and their ability to enter it, but also, and crucially, may impede the effective reallocation of resources within the economy due to the particular role of the state in network and finance sectors.

Table 6.1. Kazakhstan's results on low-level PMR indicators

2018 PMR indicators, relative to OECD average

High-level PMR indicators	Medium-level PMR indicators	Low-level PMR indicators	Kazakhstan's score relative to OECD average (higher = less competition friendly)
Distortions Induce by State Involvement	Public Ownership	Scope of SMEs	High
		Government Involvement in Network Sectors	High
		Direct Control over Enterprises	Very high
		Governance of SOEs	Very high
	Involvement in Business Operations	Retail Price Controls and Regulations	Average
		Command and Control Regulations	Low
		Public Procurement	Average
	Simplification and Evaluation of Regulations	Assessment of Impact on Competition	Very high
		Interaction with Stakeholders	High
		Complexity of Regulatory Procedures	Average

Barriers to Domestic and Foreign	Administrative Burden on Start-Ups	Admin. Burdens for JSCs and for Personally Owned Enterprises	Low
		Licenses and Permits	Average
	Barriers in Service and Network Sectors	Barriers in Service Sectors	Average
		Barriers in Network Sectors	Very high
	Barriers to Trade and Investment	Barriers to FDI	Average
		Tariff Barriers	High
		Differential Treatment of Foreign Suppliers	Very high
		Barriers to Trade Facilitation	Very high

Note: Categories are defined as "Very High" = PMR score higher than the OECD average + 2*OECD standard deviation; "High" = PMR score higher than the OECD average + OECD standard deviation
Source: (OECD, 2018[11])

The high-level, economy-wide indicator for Kazakhstan suggests that the country's overall product market regulation creates high barriers to competition, with this likely to have an impact on the general investment attractiveness of the economy. As detailed in Table 6.1 and discussed below, a key driver of the relatively weak performance in the OECD PMRs are issues relating to distortions to the playing field induced by state involvement in the economy. On these sub-indicators, Kazakhstan is significantly weaker than the OECD average, and more in line with other emerging-market economies such as Turkey and South Africa.

Figure 6.8. OECD Indicators of Product Market Regulation: Economy-wide rating (2018)

Index scale 0 to 6 from least to most restrictive

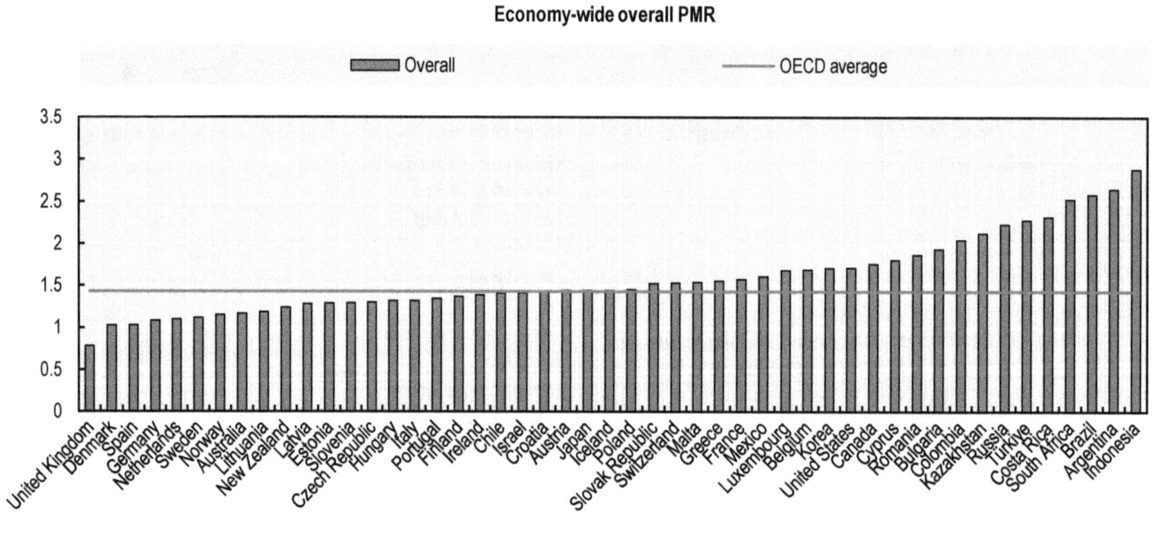

Source: (OECD, 2018[12])

The PMRs point to a number of issues relating to state involvement in the economy that may undermine the attractiveness of the economy and mitigate the potentially positive impact of its regulatory openness on potential investors' decisions. The Distortions Induced by State Involvement sub-components of public ownership, simplification and evaluation of regulations, and involvement in business operations all point to areas where Kazakhstan could yet make significant progress. At the higher-level aggregate of these three sub-components, Kazakhstan emerges as the fourth most restrictive economy in the sample covered by the OECD (Figure 6.9 a). At the medium-level component of public ownership, the country is the second most restrictive in the (Figure 6.9 b).

Figure 6.9. OECD Indicators of Product Market Regulation: Distortions Induced by State Involvement and Public Ownership (2018)

Index scale 0 to 6 from least to most restrictive

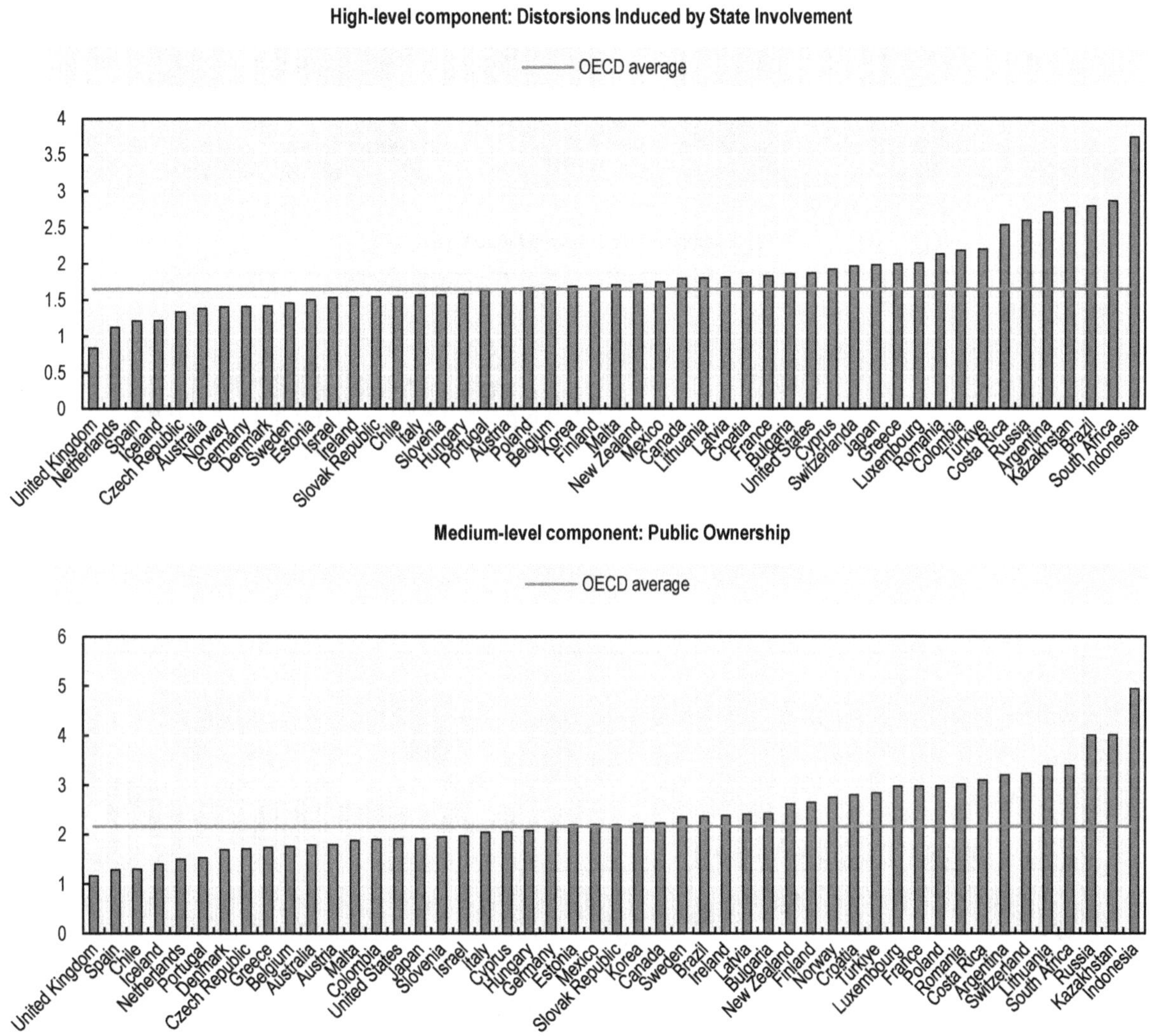

Source: (OECD, 2018[12])

The state owns at least one company in the 16 main economic sectors out of 25 analysed in the questionnaire that is used to determine a country's PMR score, including a number of firms in the manufacturing sectors and financial services (Figure 6.10 a). The government holds equity stakes in the biggest company in most of the key network sectors (gas, electricity, rail, air and water transport), with a number of the dominant firms in network sectors fully-controlled by the government (Figure 6.10 b). Direct control of firms in the economy is extensive (Figure 6.10 c), but particularly troublesome is the poor quality of governance of the country's SOEs, where Kazakhstan has the lowest PMR score of the countries included in the indicator (Figure 6.10 d).

Figure 6.10. OECD Indicators of Product Market Regulation: Low-level components on public ownership

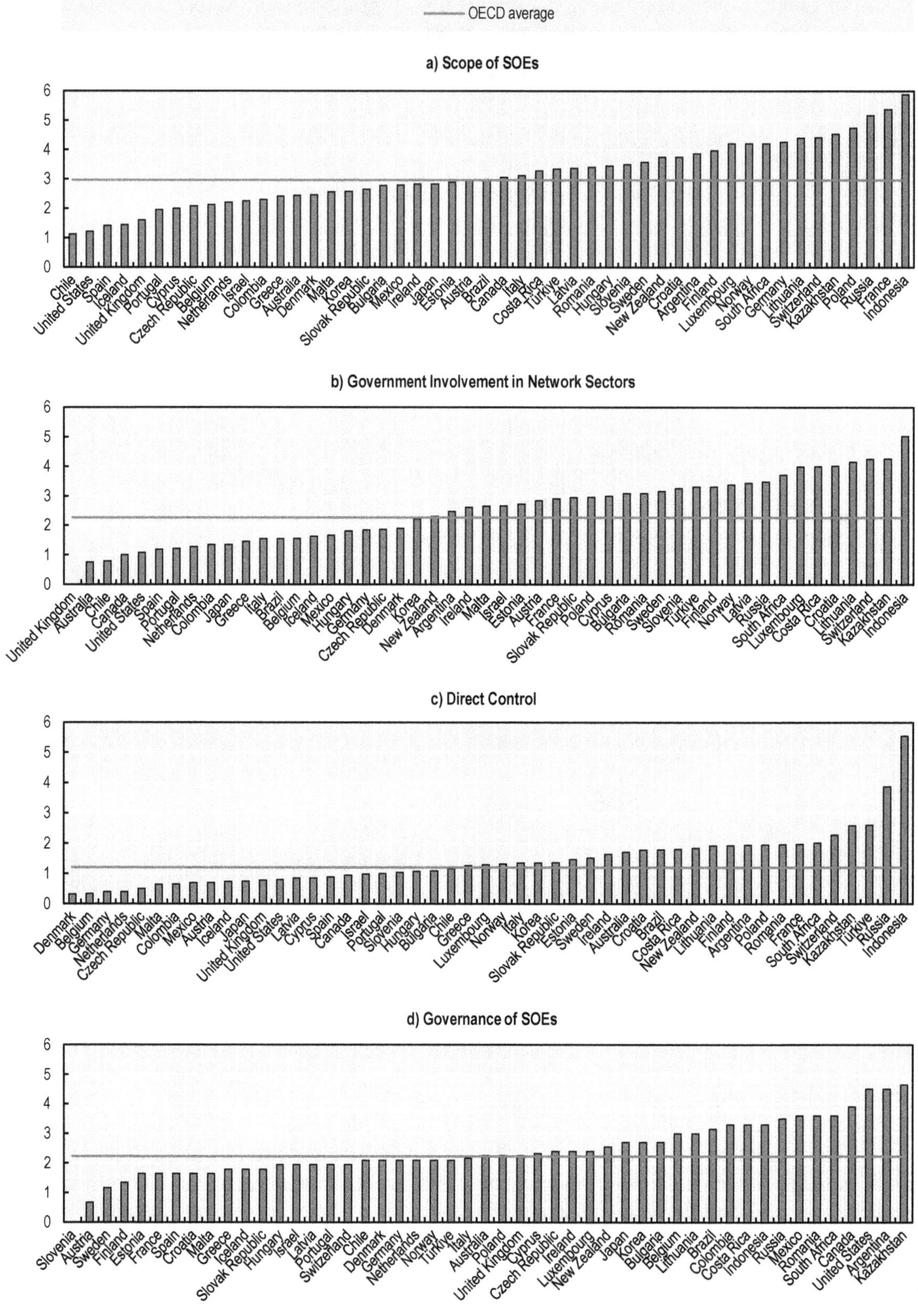

Note: Index scale 0 to 6 from least to most restrictive
Source: (OECD, 2018[12])

The high competition-related barriers to operating in a range of economic sectors are likely to act as *de facto* barriers to entry. A foreign investor may legally have the right to enter a given sector or industry, but the pervasive involvement of the state is likely to mean that it will not be able to compete fairly. The PMRs therefore highlight the fact that below a strong *de jure* environment for foreign investment, transversal and at times structural issues with a material impact on the investment climate persist.

References

Ageleuov, G. (2021), *The significance of the land issue has not yet been realized by the authorities of Kazakhstan*, Central Asian Bureau for Analytical Reporting, https://cabar.asia/en/the-significance-of-the-land-issue-has-not-yet-been-realized-by-the-authorities-of-kazakhstan. [10]

IEA (2022), *Environmental Code of the Republic of Kazakhstan, No. 400-VI*, IEA Publishing, Paris, https://www.iea.org/policies/12917-environmental-code-of-the-republic-of-kazakhstan-400-vi-as-amended. [8]

Kazakh Invest (2022), *Government has Considered and Approved Draft of the Concept of the Investment Policy of the Republic of Kazakhstan until 2026*, Government of Kazakhstan, Astana, https://invest.gov.kz/media-center/press-releases/novuyu-kontseptsiyu-investpolitiki-kazakhstana-do-2026-goda-utverdili-v-pravitelstve/. [1]

Mistura, F. and C. Roulet (2019), *The determinants of Foreign Direct Investment: Do statutory restrictions matter?*, OECD Working Papers on International Investment, OECD Publishing, Paris, https://www.oecd-ilibrary.org/docserver/641507ce-en.pdf?expires=1680263470&id=id&accname=ocid84004878&checksum=48B97299ACB63862176343291429BCFF. [4]

OECD (2023), *OECD FDI Regulatory Restrictiveness Index*, OECD Publishing, Paris, https://stats.oecd.org/Index.aspx?datasetcode=FDIINDEX. [5]

OECD (2022), *Kazakhstan (2022)*, OECD Services Trade Restrictiveness Index (STRI), OECD Publishing, Paris, https://www.oecd.org/trade/topics/services-trade/documents/oecd-stri-country-note-kaz.pdf. [6]

OECD (2021), *Improving the Legal Environment for Business and Investment in Central Asia*, OECD Publishing, Paris, https://www.oecd.org/eurasia/Improving-LEB-CA-ENG%2020%20April.pdf. [2]

OECD (2019), "OECD FDI regulatory restrictiveness index (Edition 2019)", *OECD International Direct Investment Statistics* (database), https://doi.org/10.1787/d22baa23-en (accessed on 25 April 2023). [16]

OECD (2018), *OECD Indicators of Product Market Regulation*, OECD Publishing, Paris, https://stats.oecd.org/Index.aspx?DataSetCode=PMR2018. [12]

OECD (2018), *Reforming Kazakhstan: Progress, Challenges and Opportunities*. [7]

OECD (2018), *The Regulation of Goods and Services in Kazakhstan: An International Comparison in 2018*, OECD Publishing, Paris, https://www.oecd.org/eurasia/countries/The-Regulation-of-Goods-and-Services-Markets-in-Kazakhstan.pdf. [11]

OECD (n.d.), *OECD Investment Policy Reviews*, OECD Publishing, Paris, https://doi.org/10.1787/19900910. [9]

Prime Minister Office of Kazakhstan (2019), *Over 15 million public services rendered by Government for citizens in the first half of 2019*, https://www.government.kz/en/news/press/bolee-15-mln-gosuslug-okazano-pravitelstvom-dlya-grazhdan-v-i-polugodii-2019-goda-a-ospanov. [13]

Republic of Kazakhstan (2020), *State Corporation 'Citizen Government' Online One Stop Shop*, https://egov.kz/cms/en/information/about/help-elektronnoe-pravitelstvo (accessed on 7 July 2020). [14]

Republic of Kazakhstan (2019), *Law on Legal Acts*, http://adilet.zan.kz/eng/docs/Z1600000480. [3]

World Bank (2019), *Doing Business 2019*, https://doi.org/10.1016/j.jebo.2017.07.011. [15]

www.ingramcontent.com/pod-product-compliance
Lightning Source LLC
Chambersburg PA
CBHW061223240926
51846CB00006B/1336
* 9 7 8 9 2 6 4 9 5 2 5 2 2 *